What Your Colleagues

Chen Schechter provides a refreshing lens for examining and learning from past events by showing what is made possible when teams focus on success rather than harp on failure. If you're looking to improve the school improvement process, this thought-provoking text just might be the impetus for shifting mindsets from a deficit- to an assets-based model.

—Jenni Donohoo
Co-author, *Quality Implementation: Leveraging Collective Efficacy to Make "What Works" Actually Work*

Roland Barth once pondered, out loud, how many children's lives might be saved if teachers were to disclose what they know to one another. Chen Schechter highlights the importance of collective learning among educators, proposing a process by which teachers share their wisdom. This wisdom is gleaned through reflection, especially through the framework of learning from success.

—Megan Tschannen-Moran
Professor of Educational Leadership, College of William & Mary, VA
Author, *Trust Matters: Leadership for Successful Schools*

If you were to read just one book on change in schools, professional learning communities, or establishing a positive school culture based on teaching successes, then you need to look no further. *The Collective Wisdom of Practice* gives readers a comprehensive, thoughtful, and believable guideline that takes lesson study a step further by demonstrating that the improvements of the clearly focused Learning-From-Success program is applicable in all schools.

—Dr. Neil MacNeill
Headmaster
Ellenbrook Independent Primary School, WA, Australia

Anyone interested in school improvement will benefit from the wisdom of Chen Schechter's wise analysis in this important volume.

—Sam Wineburg
Margaret Jacks Professor of Education and History
Stanford University, CA

The Collective Wisdom of Practice is a long overdue solution for schools in this era of school negativity. As professionals, we all look at improving what we do by reflecting on what works—our successes. So, the obvious question is, why doesn't this occur at a school level? The foundation of this book and the way forward is to do just this. A detailed approach is provided that any school can implement, anywhere.

—Dr. Ken Darvall
Principal
Tema International School, Ghana

The Collective Wisdom of Practice explores a Learning-From-Success model that is powerful and transformational and will encourage schools that move forward based on identified and proven successes.

—Laura Schaffer Metcalfe, EdD
Director, Early College Programs and Outreach
Mesa Community College, AZ

The Learning-From-Success model presented in *The Collective Wisdom of Practice* acknowledges that there are many things right about our schools and that we can learn as many lessons from these bright spots as we can from the challenges we have faced. Chen Schechter takes us step by step, guiding a thorough analysis of an event or situation, and concludes with lessons learned in an actionable frame and language, making it possible to apply those lessons in the future. This book teaches us how to use our learning and celebrate what is true and good about our schools.

—Shannon Hobbs-Beckley
Director of Teaching & Learning
Graded American School of Sao Paulo, Brazil

PLCs are often largely focused on talk rather than action, and the denial, avoidance, and defensiveness that often inhibit the effectiveness of teacher collaboration. However, this book represents a paradigm shift from learning from our failures to learning from our successes. *The Collective Wisdom of Practice* is a must-read for school principals and for district administrative teams.

—Melanie Mares Sainz
ESOL Teacher
Lowndes County Schools, GA

The Collective Wisdom of Practice provides the necessary information and practical guidance for any school wishing to make positive changes.

—Melissa Miller
Math and Science Instructor
Farmington Middle School, AR

The Collective
Wisdom of Practice

To my parents, Rina and Isaac Schechter, who granted me a meaningful life.

To my wife Ayelet, together in the journey to Ithaca.

To my daughters, Daria and Eileil: Every day I cherish the magical moments with you.

The Collective Wisdom of Practice

Leading Our Professional Learning From Success

Chen Schechter

Forewords by Ellie Drago-Severson and Stephanie Hirsh

A Joint Publication

FOR INFORMATION:

Corwin

A SAGE Company

2455 Teller Road

Thousand Oaks, California 91320

(800) 233-9936

www.corwin.com

SAGE Publications Ltd.

1 Oliver's Yard

55 City Road

London EC1Y 1SP

United Kingdom

SAGE Publications India Pvt. Ltd.

B 1/I 1 Mohan Cooperative Industrial Area

Mathura Road, New Delhi 110 044

India

SAGE Publications Asia-Pacific Pte. Ltd.

18 Cross Street #10-10/11/12

China Square Central

Singapore 048423

Program Director and Publisher: Dan Alpert

Content Development Editor: Lucas Schleicher

Senior Editorial Assistant: Mia Rodriguez

Production Editor: Amy Schroller

Copy Editor: Erin Livingston

Typesetter: C&M Digitals (P) Ltd.

Proofreader: Victoria Reed-Castro

Indexer: Robie Grant

Cover Designer: Scott Van Atta

Marketing Manager: Sharon Pendergast

Printed in the United States of America

ISBN 978-1-5443-8520-4

This book is printed on acid-free paper.

SFI label applies to text stock

19 20 21 22 23 10 9 8 7 6 5 4 3 2 1

Contents

 Visit the companion website at
https://resources.corwin.com/WisdomofPractice
for downloadable resources.

List of Tables and Figures

Foreword

By Ellie Drago-Severson

It is a great honor to write this foreword for my colleague, Chen Schechter. In this book, *The Collective Wisdom of Practice: Leading Our Professional Learning From Success*, Chen Schechter shares wisdom born from his deep experiences with educators in schools and systems, his knowledge of individual and organizational development, his scholarship, his research studies, and his heart. In this way, the book brings theory, research, experience, knowledge, and *wisdom* to life in service to making the world a better place for all.

To do this, Schechter takes all of us on a learning journey. This journey, like many wisdom quests, invites you to bring theoretical ideas to inform and strengthen your practice. Educators across all levels will benefit from a slow read of this work, which presents a model for Learning-From-Success—a gateway to creating the conditions for authentic learning among teachers and administrators. Schechter wisely reminds us that, while there is a clear sequence to Learning-From-Success, this kind of learning is not linear, and it takes time to employ. The time invested into this endeavor will be valuable and worth it, he argues, and I too encourage you to stay the course.

Indeed, this work is important for many reasons—among them is the fact that supporting adults in their learning, their *authentic* learning, has been proven to have a direct and positive effect on student learning and achievement. Not only is this book a must read for that reason, but also because we need to find better ways in our increasingly complex world to meet the adaptive and technical challenges that we face each day as educators. Doing so is something we cannot do alone. Throughout this book, as Schechter guides us through the model, he implicitly and explicitly shines light on a resounding truth: we need each other to learn and grow.

At its heart, the Learning-From-Success model also hinges on the importance of learning not only from our problems and challenges—as traditionally has been the case in organizations—but also and especially from our successes.

In our interconnected world, we share many common challenges, but we also share numerous hopes and opportunities. For example, in this age of the new normal, teaming and collaboration among adults are part of the fabric of our lives—our professional and personal lives. In addition, adaptive challenges are on the rise for all of us in schools, systems, and in life. In this mid 21st-century we need to find better ways to help each other learn and grow, and taking time to notice what is going well today—as we strive for ongoing improvement—can help us find our footing and foundation as we build toward new tomorrows.

Toward this end, Schechter shares lessons learned from implementing the Learning-From-Success model in a variety of settings with educators from around the world. He shares excerpts from their experiences working together and foregrounds the importance of allocating time for authentic, collaborative work. One of the many gifts of this book is that Schechter sheds light on common joys, obstacles, and hopes of educators and demonstrates how the *Learning-From-Success* model can help strengthen genuine collaboration, build communication, improve instruction, and in turn enhance student learning.

Learning Forward, a preeminent organization for supporting the learning of adults in schools and districts, has put forth a set of Standards for Professional Learning that guide us in our work supporting adults in schools. The model that Schechter has created brings these standards to life. It is grounded in best practice, research, and learning theories. For example, research has consistently shown that learning for adults in schools and systems must be ongoing, embedded in the work and practice of schools, and must include coaching. The model introduced here is one that lives these principles of best practices for supporting adults in authentic learning. Throughout this book, Schechter shares the sense making of educators across levels—teachers, principals, and others. Their stories and heartfelt experiences of collaboration, decision making, and intentionally carving out time to learn bring the importance of the model and the need for it front and center.

In addition, the Learning-From-Success model is one that focuses on how educators within schools *make sense* of their experiences of success and challenge. This, Schechter rightly argues, is especially important since "the expertise of educational practitioners in schools is a rich, barely tapped resource" (p. 78). He also points out that, all too often, "due to systemic bias toward learning from difficulties or failures, successes in schools have rarely been the object of deliberative collective learning" (p. 78). And, this final point, which is both the inspiration for the book and the model, is the hope of capitalizing on wisdom: "For the expertise that underlies success to be tapped, it must undergo a process (learning from success) through which educators' tacit knowledge is transformed into school knowledge, thus assisting faculty members in verifying, sorting, and filtering data" (p. 78).

With these guiding principles, Schechter shines light on a truism that you may be familiar with: namely, that the wisdom is, indeed, in the room. He gives us a guide for accessing wisdom that matters and that stems from within. This model enables us not only to reach deeply within ourselves, but also offers us a framework for listening deeply to others and how they are making sense of their experiences. This matters. This matters in schools, in collaboration, in relationships with students and with colleagues. This matters in life.

The importance of these features and the Learning-From-Success model itself has been field-tested in several contexts including at the national level. In this book, Schechter not only draws from his research with educators and administrators in diverse settings that mirror the complexity of education around the globe, but he also includes rich case studies that shed light on the work of three diverse schools, which were part of an initiative supported by the Israeli Ministry of Education.

In these cases, Schechter carefully and caringly illustrates real-life examples of how others have improved their practice and their capacities for collaboration and collective learning by implementing this step-by-step, systematic set of processes. He shines light on the why, the how, and the who in this volume—*and* grounds these practical examples in rich theoretical context. Schechter does this by illuminating his own and other scholars' findings from research about the principles which underlie the Learning-From-Success model. In other words, he helps us understand the organizational, individual, internal, and theoretical implications and possibilities of the model.

Ultimately, learning how to learn collectively, to collaborate authentically, and to learn from our successes as well as our problems takes time. It takes courage. It takes creating the conditions so that this kind of authentic collaboration can grow and become part of the fabric of our teacher teams, our vertical teams, and our leadership teams—or, as Schechter refers to them, Leading Forums.

Reflecting on this transformative vision, I'm reminded of a recent success that I had the privilege of witnessing. I had the honor of working with a group of principals in a district with high poverty and low resources and I was guiding principals as they were trying to learn about and practice a developmental approach to feedback, so that they and all educators in their school communities could get better at collaborating and communicating and helping each other grow. At the end of the year-long program, one of the district leaders addressed the group of principals. He offered the following with love and out of care in his closing remarks to the large group of all of the principals in this district and the district level team:

> I know that we love when we can learn something quickly and implement it immediately so that we can see results in a short period of time. The work that we've been doing this year [around implementing this model] is going to be work that we continue to do this year, next year, and the year after in order for it to grow in our schools so that we can continue to raise student achievement and improve as a district. We need to hold each

other accountable in implementation in order for that to happen. We need to check in with each other about how it's going. We need to talk about the successes and the challenges of implementing [this model] and help each other.

This district leader's wisdom echoes the message of Schechter's work. We know that there is no *one* way to make the world a better place. There is no *one* way to increase student achievement. There is no *one* way to build schools. We need to plant many seeds and nurture them simultaneously in order for any of these things to happen. It is a process that requires our strength, courage, vulnerability, passion, patience, and love. In the same way, we must grow our muscles for *Learning-From-Success*—for our children, for ourselves, for our schools, and for our world. This is the promise of this book. This is our hope. Let us join together and journey forward with this hope.

—Ellie Drago-Severson
Professor of Education Leadership & Adult Learning and Leadership
Director, Leadership Institute for School Change
Teachers College, Columbia University

Foreword

By Stephanie Hirsh

"You have to get Mrs. Thomas for fourth grade; she is amazing!"

"Make sure Seth takes Mrs. Clay for English; she will make sure he is ready for college."

I know that words of advice like these can be heard in friendly conversations everywhere. Among parents' greatest concerns at the beginning of the school year is knowing their children will have the best teachers possible. While parents may not be familiar with the evidence base, they know teachers matter. A teacher can make or break a student's—and a family's—year.

Parents are also very generous in recognizing that different teachers have different strengths. It is not uncommon to hear comments like, "I wish my daughter had a teacher with the passion of Miss Yu and the content expertise of Dr. Ponder."

Like all of us, teachers are unique human beings with their own strengths and areas for growth. Fortunately, working in the learning profession positions them to learn from their successes as well as their failures. This is why I am excited for the release of *The Collective Wisdom of Practice: Leading Our Professional Learning From Success* and its focus on building on the strengths of the teachers in a school.

Ideally parents and students would have the benefit of the expertise of all the teachers in a school, grade level, or subject area. Schools organized so that every educator deliberately learns from success can make this ideal a reality for more students, families, and educators. It's one thing to acknowledge this fact; it's another to put those aspirations into practice. Chen Schechter provides a research grounded, accessible approach to integrating learning from success into the daily routines of educators.

When I served on a local school board, the one question I found most difficult to answer was a friend's request to help them convince a principal to put their child in a particular teacher's classroom. Of course, I knew it was not my role as a school board member to make that request, and yet I wanted so much to be able to give this answer to my friend:

> While it is inappropriate for me to make this request, what I can assure is that your child's school is a learning school. This means that every teacher is learning every day with the sole purpose of getting better at their job and ensuring the success of every student. At your child's school, every grade level or department shares collective responsibility for the success of all the students in the building. And what this means for your child is that no matter what door she enters on that first day of school, you can be assured that she will experience the same powerful teaching and learning experiences as any other child in the school. This means that when your child is struggling, all the teachers will work together to find the solution. I am confident your child is going to have a fabulous year at this learning school.

The fact is, I would only be able to say that about schools that had embraced collective responsibility for all students as a core value. Collective responsibility for the success of all students helps all teachers become the best they can be. What I most appreciate about Chen Schechter's vision for school transformation is that collective responsibility sits in its heart.

Collective responsibility can be merely a phrase in a school vision, mission, or theory of action. Or it can be translated into commitments and actions that can be demonstrated and affirmed by educators in schools. Consider these elements and the actions demonstrated by those who embrace its meaning.

Collective responsibility means that all staff members are committed to ensuring every student has the best teaching and learning experience possible no matter what classroom they sit in. They are building strong relationships with all students and their families in their grade level or subject matter. In addition, they look for opportunities to get to know the students they will serve next year or next semester. When a teacher learns that any student is struggling and they have information or strategies that can help, they feel a responsibility to share their wisdom. When approached with such information, teachers and others are grateful and ready to change. Everyone celebrates when things are going well and commits to making changes when they are not achieving their goals. Strong relationships with several educators are a powerful foundation for success of all students.

Collective responsibility means that every teacher has a support system. In these schools no teacher or other staff member is allowed to fail in his or her efforts to ensure success for any one student. In schools that embrace collective responsibility staff members commit to the team approach to solving problems. Everyone is a member of at least one team. Teachers and other staff members understand, support, and appreciate the benefits of working collaboratively. Whenever one teacher is facing a challenge, the team is there for support.

Collective responsibility means all students experience great lessons and effective assessments every day. Students benefit from the wisdom and expertise of all teachers in a grade level or subject. It also means that every student is graded by the same standards as all other students in the same grade level or course. Collective responsibility means a shared commitment to students experiencing consistently high-quality teaching and learning every day.

Collective responsibility means teachers regularly share what is working in their classroom with their colleagues. Data are transparent and teachers experiencing success are easily identified. Opportunities to share new learning are systematically scheduled, studied, and celebrated. Teachers have different strengths and areas of expertise; they are celebrated when they have success and eager to praise and learn from colleagues who experience success in other areas. Best practices spread from classroom to classroom.

Collective responsibility means teachers with less experience seek support from more experienced teachers. New teachers appreciate that other teachers are invested in their success and the success of all students. Mentors, buddies, and team members serve new teachers in different ways. One may provide emotional support for overcoming the challenges teachers face early in their career. One might teach the culture and traditions of the school. One may support planning for all the big firsts of a new teacher, including first days, first parent conferences, and first assessments. And one might ensure the new teacher feels supported year-round with access to great materials, assessments, and expertise. From day one, all teachers know that their responsibility goes beyond the walls of the classroom they are assigned.

Collective responsibility means teachers open their doors to their colleagues, coaches, and principal. They recognize the tremendous value in the perspectives and insights of others. They understand the importance of multiple views in decision making to support students. They may seek feedback on a new strategy, new perspectives on student engagement, or insight on classroom culture. They trust their colleagues' intentions and professional judgment. They respect the expertise they bring to the conversations.

Collective responsibility means teachers learn and work together systematically on a regular schedule. Time for teacher learning is a priority in the school schedule. It is protected for application of the school's learning cycle. They recognize the importance of a deep dive into their data so they can understand their students as well as their own learning needs. They set goals together for individuals and groups of students and determine what they must learn in order to facilitate the success they want for their students. They identify members of their learning team with demonstrated expertise in their priority learning areas. They establish a learning agenda that details the actions they will take to develop appropriate knowledge and skills including learning from the experts on their team, in their school as well as beyond their school community. As learning progresses, they study their curriculum to identify places where they anticipate students may struggle and how they will support them; where they will incorporate their new learning and skills; and when they will be transferring their learning into the classroom with students. They review and or develop new assessments and establish a plan for monitoring the progress of their students. Experience with consistent application of the cycle affirms its value in supporting their growth and student progress.

Finally, **collective responsibility means** that teachers can count on principals and district offices recognizing the expertise that lies within schools. Systems that promote collective responsibility hold the value that the vast majority of problems can be solved by the individuals within schools when given the appropriate support and supervision. They have tremendous respect for the educators with direct responsibility for the success of students. They see it as their responsibility to ensure that educators have what they need to promote ongoing growth. This includes prioritizing the time and support required for meaningful engagement in effective learning teams. This includes modeling the collaboration and professional learning they want from others. This means elevating the expertise and success in classrooms and making sure it moves from classroom to classroom and school to school.

When all of our students learn in schools that embrace learning and collective responsibility, I am confident we'll see the level of transformation that signal a new era for student learning—an era where gaps between students of different backgrounds and circumstances disappear and wisdom and expertise are shared openly and daily. I'm eager to watch Chen Schechter's contribution to this future assist educators. Cultures, structures, and habits will change in schools that embrace his strategies.

—Stephanie Hirsh
Former Executive Director of Learning Forward

Preface

In schools, we often target failures, and we try to design curricula, programs, and activities around how to overcome our students' shortcomings rather than focusing on and learning from what they are doing well.

—a high school teacher

Every time I visit one of the schools under my supervision, I ask the principal and his/her staff to write down all the problems at school, so I can help them solve these problems. I never thought to ask for their successes as a mode for collective learning.

—a school district superintendent

The traditional education systems are collapsing.

Schools today are dangerous and violent places.

Students are not becoming equipped to succeed in higher learning and in the world of work.

Many groups in our country do not get the education they need and deserve.

We are continuously losing our best and most creative teachers.

—the voices of parents, teachers, and the media

These disappointed and concerned voices, expressing dissatisfaction from what is or is not transpiring in today's schools, can be easily overheard from parents and teachers alike around the world, as often echoed in the media and at academic conferences. In contrast, voices are rarely heard describing schools' success stories and teachers' effective actions and triumphs in preparing students for the global challenges they face in the 21st century.

The education system's importance cannot be overestimated: Within that system, each of us begins life's journey, acquiring the knowledge and tools necessary for integrating into our own challenging society, wherever it is in the world, and for internalizing its values. The education system is also a crucial apparatus that facilitates the development and prosperity of that society's collective interests, steadily reflecting its democratic humanistic values and continuously imparting these skills and values to the next generation. At the same time, it is difficult to exaggerate the severity of its problems: The western education system is all too often characterized by poor scholastic achievements, relatively low rates of students who qualify for matriculation certificates, widening gaps between various subgroups in the population, many cases of violence, overcrowded classrooms, outdated teaching methods and infrastructure, and more.

To counter these problems, education policies in many western countries have primarily centered on the infiltration of market-based approaches into education. Such market-based policies—for example, No Child Left Behind, Race To The Top (with the double-meaning of *race*), and Common Core Standards reforms in the United States—have steered education priorities toward regimes of standardized testing and accountability, attaching high-stakes consequences to the results of external and comparative tests (Fullan, 2016; Hargreaves & Fullan, 2012). These high-stakes top-down educational policies have narrowed the definition of *educational success* to focus solely on schools' achievement levels rather than on professionals' and students' growth, often resulting in student disengagement and dropout, racial or cultural disparities in academic outcomes, and attrition of the best teachers (e.g., Darling-Hammond, Meyerson, La Pointe, & Orr, 2010).

The growing tendency for top-down reforms that attempt to solve the education system's severe problems by focusing on schools' high-stakes accountability for student achievement echoes Einstein's broadly credited quote of defining *insanity* as doing the same thing over and over again while expecting different results. Critics of the U.S. education system's "amnesia" have repeatedly argued that this market-based high-stakes standards model of learning and growth discourages school leaders, teachers, and especially our children from nurturing their individual capabilities and collective wisdoms (e.g., Ravitch's *Reign of Errors*, 2014). It slowly but surely blinds us from seeing how teachers and students can grow and succeed through learning communities committed to continuous bottom-up improvement, collective responsibility, and goal alignment (Learning Forward, 2018).

In light of our continuous seductive dance with these top-down market-based and high-stakes standards approaches, what lies ahead for our school systems? As accountability and competition have permeated schools and transformed them into service marketplaces for students and families (Blackmore, 2006), sidetracking issues of equity and social justice, can we shift toward more democratic collectivism of our school systems? Can we forecast a trajectory of school learning that will be based on a more holistic and positive way to address the complexity of school life? Can educators deliberate on their successful practices as leverage for continually nurturing the practical wisdom necessary to work in dynamic school contexts? Can we envision learning practices in schools that co-create a rich, multifaceted vision based on diverse perspectives and divergent values? Can learning move from exclusion to inclusion and even reciprocity? In particular, can learning bottom-up from schools' own "professional wisdom"—teachers' own experiences, knowledge, and good judgment reflecting what actually works in practice (Argyris & Schon, 1996)—better serve 21st-century educators than market-based reforms imposed from the top down in schools? Is bottom-up learning from professional wisdom particularly important when implementing complex and dynamic processes across high-stakes improvement cycles and turnaround efforts in an increasingly globalized and interactive learning milieu?

"Give me a lever long enough and a fulcrum on which to place it, and I shall move the world," said Archimedes. How much momentum will be needed to make these meaningful and necessary changes? Can we employ better levers for change in a seductive era of top-down market-based approaches in education? Does the fulcrum on which the educational system rests support the above possible trajectories of positive, inclusive, and reciprocal learning and growth?

Since the early 19th century, Taylor's (1911) principles of scientific administration have dominated the procedures and structures of public schools, involving principles of top-down division of labor, hierarchy, and control over the school organization. This mechanistic view of schools has been sharply criticized (e.g., Giles & Hargreaves, 2006; Hord, 2016). For the most part, criticism has focused on such procedures' and structures' inadequacy in providing practitioners with opportunities, spaces, and means for carrying out important shared dialogue and cooperation with other practitioners in the system (Louis, 2006; Lu & Hallinger, 2018; Mulford & Silins, 2011; Schechter, 2012). Increasingly, scholars have strongly advocated that public school teachers, who mostly work in isolation, must take steps toward interactive professionalism, where teachers continuously deliberate together on how to solve problems that relate to teaching and learning (DuFour & DuFour, 2013; Fullan, 2016).

To survive, and certainly to thrive in turbulent and uncertain environments, teachers must learn to learn, thereby developing their own abilities to engage in ongoing learning of skills for effective teaching. One way of doing so is to recognize the importance of learning as a continuous collective process—and act upon it. In order to overcome the complexities they face, educators must introduce and then maintain continuous social processes that engender their own learning, through which they can become members of collective interpretation systems. Hence, sharing and generating multiple interpretations with peers in regard to the school's professional practices can help practitioners do justice to their professional mission.

Inasmuch as traditional hierarchical models of school administration contrast with the advocated value of social exchange, various initiatives have been undertaken to reorganize schools into professional webs of interactions. Such efforts were expected to enhance professional development, which, in turn, may help to break down teachers' isolation barriers, to alter teaching practices, and to contribute to student learning (Hord, 2016). Nevertheless, collective learning has seldom been translated into sustained structures and processes in school reality (Schechter, 2011c, 2012). Thus, faculty members remain in need of practical frameworks to assist them in negotiating their professional practices—which comprise their precious professional wisdoms.

There is much promise in focusing on collective learning from past school experiences (retrospective learning) to elicit educators' wisdom of practice. Put simply, learning from past experiences is of the utmost importance, as educators strive to have a positive impact on their students. Somewhat surprisingly, as far as examining past events as opportunities for learning and growth in schools, this has traditionally been focused on failures and difficulties, whereas successful events and processes have remained relatively unexamined. The primary focus on retrospective learning from failed events and processes not only skews teachers' discourse in a negative direction but also deprives teachers of learning opportunities embedded in past successes and satisfactory events. Although learning from success has been perceived as the enemy of experimentation and innovation, the deliberate choice to learn from school stakeholders' successful experiences can serve as leverage for future integration of collective learning both from successes and from failures and from all that lies between (Schechter, 2010, 2011b).

The idea of learning from successful professional practices has long been advocated by Rosenfeld and his associates as one of the ways in which human service professionals can move beyond impasses in the service of their clients, especially those who have been marginalized (Rosenfeld, 1997; Rosenfeld, Schon, & Sykes, 1995). Learning from success has thus been conceptualized as an essential step toward the transformation of such social service systems. It is only through a collective learning process that clarifies what it takes to provide "good enough" services that an organization can redesign structures, policy, research, evaluation, and training so that they actively support and promote these "successful" forms of work.

Facing ever-increasing pressure to transform school systems into dynamic learning environments, school leaders and educators find their roles becoming more and more complex (Fullan, 2014; Organization for Economic Co-operation and Development, 2016; Schleicher, 2012). As schools are expected to demonstrate both excellence and equity as means for improving teaching and learning for all students in the system, learning from success has the power to transform teachers' discourse toward sharing their own excellent and equitable practices. The deliberate and conscious choice to collaboratively learn from successful practices may nurture the practical wisdom necessary for working in dynamic school contexts.

Hence, the overarching goal of this book is to present the *collective learning-from-success* approach. The main argument of this book is that educators—teachers, mid-level school leaders, principals, district leaders, and policymakers—who face contemporary pressures to transform school systems into more successful and equitable spaces for all students may benefit from the collective inquiry into their wisdoms of practice, reflecting on the actionable knowledge that made professional successes possible. In a nutshell, one teacher who participated in learning-from-success inquiry summarized the importance of this success-focused collaborative process as follows:

> The fact that your success is announced within a group of teachers and collectively analyzed is like a self-fulfilling prophecy that arouses feelings of pride. This process illuminates that each and every teacher has an important and positive role in the school. It is an essential process in building a professional team because, as we all know, teachers rarely receive positive feedback.

As can be seen in Figure P.1, which outlines the whole book's scope and contents, Chapter 1 begins this book by outlining the framework of the professional learning community as leverage upon which to situate collective learning among school professionals, suggesting the possible benefits and pitfalls that educators may face in the pursuit of such professional communities. Chapter 2 discusses the rudiments of collective retrospective learning as a built-in continuous-improvement vehicle within schools, focusing on collective professional learning communities in general and on learning from problems and successes in particular. Thus, the chapter explores the widespread human predisposition to learn from problems and failures, while pinpointing both the opportunities afforded by this problem-based form of learning as well as the obstacles it poses. This chapter then expands on the limitations and the potential benefits of learning from successful practices and positive experiences. Chapter 3 gives voice to educators' own perceptions of learning from success. This aims to not only focus on how teachers themselves perceive this form of learning but also on the necessary conditions for igniting such collaborative learning processes in school systems.

Chapter 4 leads readers into the *learning-from-success journey*—a structured multicomponent framework for collaborative inquiry into professional successes that may provide the impetus for significant change in schools. This chapter details how to enact learning from success, while describing strategies, participants, products, and evaluation processes. Offering practical guidelines and concrete tools for interested school stakeholders, Chapter 5 presents a comprehensive case study for

FIGURE P.1   The Book's Structure Along the Learning-From-Success Journey

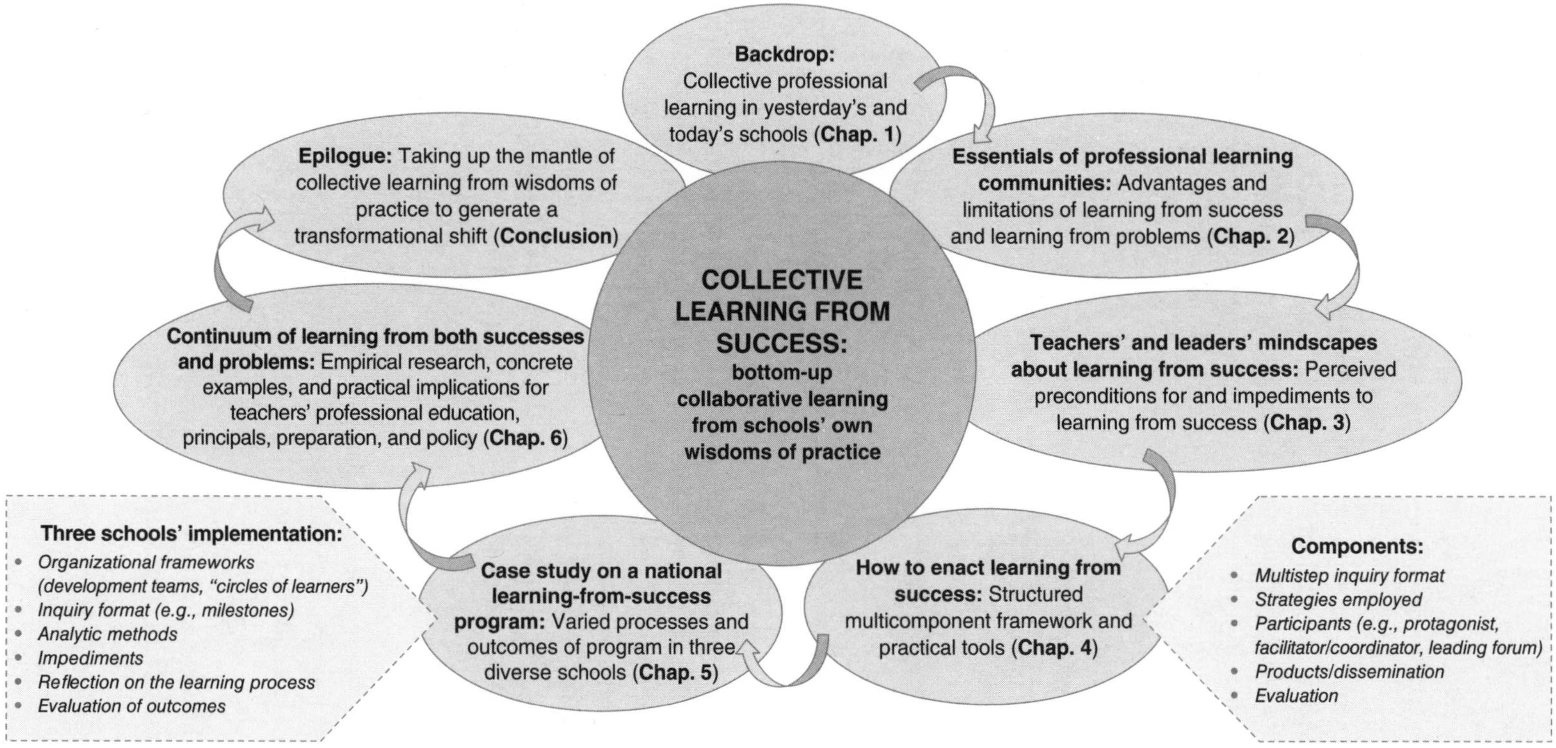

Backdrop: Collective professional learning in yesterday's and today's schools **(Chap. 1)**

Essentials of professional learning communities: Advantages and limitations of learning from success and learning from problems **(Chap. 2)**

Teachers' and leaders' mindscapes about learning from success: Perceived preconditions for and impediments to learning from success **(Chap. 3)**

COLLECTIVE LEARNING FROM SUCCESS: bottom-up collaborative learning from schools' own wisdoms of practice

How to enact learning from success: Structured multicomponent framework and practical tools **(Chap. 4)**

Case study on a national learning-from-success program: Varied processes and outcomes of program in three diverse schools **(Chap. 5)**

Continuum of learning from both successes and problems: Empirical research, concrete examples, and practical implications for teachers' professional education, principals, preparation, and policy **(Chap. 6)**

Epilogue: Taking up the mantle of collective learning from wisdoms of practice to generate a transformational shift **(Conclusion)**

Components:
- Multistep inquiry format
- Strategies employed
- Participants (e.g., protagonist, facilitator/coordinator, leading forum)
- Products/dissemination
- Evaluation

Three schools' implementation:
- Organizational frameworks (development teams, "circles of learners")
- Inquiry format (e.g., milestones)
- Analytic methods
- Impediments
- Reflection on the learning process
- Evaluation of outcomes

implementing learning from success—the National Program of Learning from Success—and discusses the organizational frameworks, inquiry processes, and outcomes of this program as illustrated in detail for three participating schools' diverging applications. Switching gears, Chapter 6 outlines the continuum of collective learning—where learning from successes and learning from failures/problems are seen as complementing and nourishing to one another regarding pedagogy and instruction. This chapter presents empirical research, examples of how teachers integrate systematic learning from problematic as well as successful experiences in their real-time classrooms, and practical implications for professional preparation and policy implementation. The Conclusion proposes the needed transformational shift toward systematic nurturing of schools' rich wisdom of practice, which already exists among isolated educators who continuously craft magical learning moments with our children, and merely awaits policymakers' and school leaders' support for sharing that vast wisdom with colleagues.

> How do you expect us to fly as you fly? came another voice.
>
> You are special and gifted and divine, above other birds.
>
> Look at Fletcher! Lowell! Charles-Roland! Are they also special and gifted and divine? No more than you are, no more than I am.
>
> The only difference, the very only one, is that they have begun to understand what they really are and have begun to practice it.
>
> His students, save Fletcher, shifted uneasily. They hadn't realized that this was what they are doing.
>
> (Bach, 1970, p. 183)

It is my hope that this book will shift educators' minds and souls to more fully understand the special, precious, and gifted pearls of wisdom that underlie what practitioners are already doing by helping them learn to share their best practices with their companions on the journey of education. Learning from each other's professional successes can nurture educators' wisdom of practice and help it soar to meet the challenges we all face in preparing our children to co-create a better future.

Acknowledgments

To Jona Rosenfeld, a true mentor, for sharing the spirit of and passion for learning from success.

To Sarit Ellenbogen-Frankovits and Israel Sykes, for their valuable thoughts on learning from success.

To my publishers, for a marvelous job: Dan Alpert, Lucas Schleicher, Mia Rodriguez, and Amy Schroller. Thank you.

PUBLISHER'S ACKNOWLEDGMENTS

Corwin gratefully acknowledges the contributions of the following reviewers:

Dr. Ken Darvall
Principal
Tema International School, Ghana

Melanie S. Hedges
NBCT, Art Teacher
West Gate Elementary School
West Palm Beach, FL

Shannon Hobbs-Beckley
Director of Teaching and Learning
Graded American School of Sao Paulo
Sao Paulo, SP, Brazil

Dr. Neil MacNeill
Head Master
Ellenbrook Independent Primary School
Ellenbrook, WA, Australia

Dr. Laura Schaffer Metcalfe
Director, Early College Programs and Outreach
Mesa Community College
Mesa, AZ

Melissa Miller
Math/Science Instructor
Farmington Middle School
Farmington, AR

Karen Mitcham
K–12 Literacy Specialist
Middle GA Regional Education Service Agency
Warner Robins, GA

Lena Marie Rockwood
High School Assistant Principal
Revere Public Schools
Revere, MA

Melanie Mares Sainz
ESOL Teacher
Lowndes County Schools
Valdosta, GA

About the Author

Chen Schechter is a professor of leadership, organizational development, and policy in education. He believes that educators need to be encouraged to embark on the exciting journey of nurturing the remarkable wisdom of practice that characterizes their magical learning moments with our children. Professor Schechter aims to build bridges and integrate theory with empirical evidence and practice by supporting teachers, principals, superintendents, and policymakers in their professional growth. His research areas include reform implementation, educational change, professional learning communities, organizational learning, collaborative learning from success, educational leadership, leadership development, and systems thinking for school leaders. Professor Schechter teaches, conducts research, and serves as a professional advisor in numerous international, national, district, and school development projects, with deep commitment to developing bottom-up school leadership and transformative learning and innovation.

Professor Schechter earned his PhD in K–12 Educational Administration and Leadership from the Ohio State University and currently serves as editor-in-chief of the Journal of Educational Administration (JEA), the oldest and most respected leading international journal in the field of educational leadership and management. Professor Schechter has published his research extensively in a wide range of highly ranked journals and has authored five recent books: *The Collective Wisdom of Practice: Leading Our Professional Learning From Success* (2020); *Leading Holistically: How Schools, Districts, and States Improve Systemically* (2018); *The NSSE Yearbook* (National Society for the Study of Education) of Columbia University's Teachers College on *Developing Models for Teaching and*

Learning Self-Regulated Learning (2017); *Systems-Thinking for School Leaders: Holistic Leadership for Excellence in Schools* (2017); and *Let Us Lead! School Principals at the Forefront of Reforms* (2015).

CHAPTER 1

Shifting Schools Toward Collaborative Learning Communities

I had thought—and believed—that our school worked as a learning community, but what I experienced was actually a lack of openness or willingness to hear different perspectives. It was like camouflage; we were sitting there together but could not express our thoughts and learn from the things we do at school.

—an elementary school teacher

A learning community can exist within an atmosphere that is both pleasant and challenging at the same time and that enables collaborative learning based on a common desire to succeed together and to create together. However, without the appropriate in-school culture, teachers could view this collaborative learning as a criticism of their work and perhaps as undermining their authority.

—an elementary school teacher

The goal of the group is not only to provide information but also to initiate new projects, to solve pedagogical problems, and to serve as a support and learning group. The goal is learning. But we really don't have time for learning because we mainly focus on receiving information, such as new projects decided by

(Continued)

administrators at the school and district levels. We are only updated with information that needs to be delivered to students, such as scheduled dates for final exams and new regulations for communicating with parents. There is no time for real learning. There is no time to delve into curricular and pedagogical issues.

—a high school teacher

These voices of teachers clearly articulate the continuous efforts to create learning communities in schools as well as the struggles in their implementation. In the current chapter, I hope to set the stage for this book's discussion of the impressive possibilities afforded by professional learning communities—especially those focusing on schools' successes—and of practical ways to help bring them to fruition in spite of possible barriers and challenges. To paraphrase Thomas Mann (*The Magic Mountain*, 1924), teachers learn not only through their own individual professional experiences but also, and more importantly—consciously or unconsciously—by learning with and from their contemporaries.

Yet, frequently, on the ground in schools, attempts to learn consciously from colleagues in the context of professional learning communities to date have largely been focused on talk rather than action and on failures rather than successes. Even those collective learning forums that ostensibly "celebrate the successes" attained in their schools do not usually zoom in on the schools' own success stories as the focus of teachers' systematic collaborative learning processes. Before delving into the potential advantages of success-based professional learning communities—the major focus of this book—and presenting practical guidelines for launching such a learning culture from scratch into uncharted or resistant schools, the current chapter offers the backdrop for examining learning-from-success practices. Looking historically and contemporarily at schools' collective learning attempts, this chapter outlines schools' important shift from the mechanistic framework to the collaborative framework of learning, discusses the main characteristics of professional learning communities, and suggests possible benefits and pitfalls in the pursuit of such communal learning.

MECHANISTIC VERSUS COLLABORATIVE VIEWS OF SCHOOLS

Let us begin our exploration of collective professional learning with a retrospective look at expectations from school organizations historically. Traditionally, schools were perceived as rational hierarchical institutions based on bureaucratic characteristics. Such expectations, nurtured during the Industrial Age, were epitomized in Charlie Chaplin's film, *Modern Times* (1936), where modern life was analogized to a factory assembly line. This mechanistic view—upholding that an effective school is divided into small, separate, well-functioning units that can be monitored and routinized for efficient performance—has been strongly criticized by researchers and practitioners alike (Hargreaves & Fullan, 2012). In such an assembly-line bureaucratic management mentality, teachers tend to work in isolation, expected to conceal their "emerging" pedagogical ideas in order to conform to the centralized policies imposed from the top downward. This deeply rooted mechanistic view characterizing the history of educational systems has resulted in schools' fragmentation into distinct classrooms and grade levels—linear organizational models that restrict mutual dialogue, deliberation, and growth.

For the most part, criticism of such organizational and leadership practices has centered on their inherent lack of both the time and the space that would allow practitioners to conduct dialogue and deliberation with one another (Louis, 2006; Schechter, 2018; Trust & Horrocks, 2017), where the supposed autonomy afforded to teachers in fact leads to their sense of disconnection and pedagogical isolation. Critics of mechanistic school practices—which continue to prevail up through today—express concern that if teachers are to be accountable for the growth and development of their students, then schools must create and sustain collaborative learning practices—learning opportunities and social exchanges that can best foster teachers' own processes of growth and development (Fullan, 2016; Stoll, McMahon, & Thomas, 2006). Louis (2006) argued that the capacity of schools to innovate and reform relies on their ability to process, understand, and apply knowledge about teaching and learning at a collective level. Scholars contend that in order for schools to revise their existing knowledge and keep pace with environmental changes, they must establish systematic structures, processes, and practices that facilitate the continuous collaborative learning of all their members (Dogan, Pringle, & Mesa, 2016; Mulford & Silins, 2011). In turn, such collaborative learning is expected to enhance professional development, which may help break down teacher isolation barriers, alter teaching practices, and contribute to student learning (Hargreaves & Fullan, 2012; Vangrieken, Meredith, Packer, & Kyndt, 2017).

Considering the extent to which traditional hierarchical models of school organization contrast with the advocated value of collaborative social exchange, researchers have argued for schools' reorganization into professional "webs" of interactions (e.g., Louis, 2006; Mitchell & Sackney, 2006; Veelen, Sleegers, & Endedijk, 2017). This recommendation calls for "re-culturing" schools into professional learning communities (DuFour, 2004; DuFour & DuFour, 2013).

What Are Professional Learning Communities?

In schools, *professional learning communities* are collaborative networks of learning processes among community members (Louis, 2006; Roy & Hord, 2006; Vollenbroek, Wetterling, & de Vries, 2017). In contrast with the prevalent fragmentation of schools into isolated so-called autonomous classrooms, in these networks, teachers can continuously deliberate with one another on how to solve problems that relate to teaching and learning (Andrews & Crowther, 2006; Mitchell & Sackney, 2006). In addition, professional learning community members share ideas, personal commitment, and a sense of professional collegiality. Social interaction within such collegial professional networks in schools can transform the image of the isolated teacher into one of "interactive professionalism" (Fullan, 2016) around issues of teaching and learning. More specifically, Bryk, Camburn, and Louis (1999); DuFour, Eaker, and Many (2006); and Roy and Hord (2006) identified the following four core characteristics of a school professional learning community:

1. *Collective learning*, consisting of reflective dialogue focusing on instruction and student learning, where teachers reflect on instructional practices and examine tacit assumptions about teaching and learning

2. *De-privatization of practice*, where teachers provide feedback through networks of professional interactions and share knowledge beyond their own classrooms (e.g., become mentors)

3. *Peer collaboration*, where teachers collaborate on school projects that focus on professional reform and improvement initiatives

4. *Shared leadership and facilitative-supportive actions* on the part of the principal and the administration

While all four of these core characteristics are interrelated and should be aligned to produce the capacity for a professional learning community, no single method can be applied to all schools wishing to create such a community. Professional learning communities are not contrived but rather emerge from the specific needs, goals, and aspirations of each community's members.

Teacher teams are the structural foundation of professional learning communities. They constitute action communities that serve as the cornerstones of the school's broad professional learning community (Opfer & Pedder, 2011; Schmoker, 2004). *Action communities* are groups of people who share a certain concern or a set of problems or a passion for a particular subject and who deepen their knowledge and expertise in this field through continuous interaction. These communities act as "social learning systems" where professionals connect to each other to solve problems, share ideas, set standards, build tools, and develop relationships with colleagues and stakeholders.

Thus, a professional learning community is fundamentally rooted in cooperation between teachers. In this process, teachers work together to analyze and improve learning and teaching in their classrooms (DuFour, 2004; Hord & Sommers, 2008). The teachers expose their own teaching methods while being receptive to colleagues' opinions, experiences, approaches, and teaching techniques. By engaging in conversation, they share what has traditionally been thought of as personal—their own goals, strategies, teaching materials, questions, concerns, and outcomes (Dufour et al., 2006). They may observe their peers' classes, offering feedback and discussing common professional issues (Bolam, McMahon, Stoll, Thomas, & Wallace, 2005). This joint culture encourages teachers (who are mostly accustomed to working autonomously) to shift toward teamwork (McLaughlin & Talbert, 2006).

Moreover, *reflective investigation* is part of the professional learning community's process. Within the collective framework, teachers regularly conduct reflective dialogues that critically examine their modes of practice against the goals they have set for themselves in accordance with their vision. Interaction between teachers with different sorts of knowledge and experiences provides opportunities for learning and critical reflection (Greene, 2007), which, in turn, creates shared knowledge of professional practices. Thus, the professional learning community can also be defined as "a school organization in which a group of teachers share and question their practices. . . . This questioning happens in an ongoing, reflective, collaborative, and inclusive way" (De Neve, Devos, & Tuytens, 2015, p. 32).

POTENTIAL BENEFITS AND PITFALLS OF PROFESSIONAL LEARNING COMMUNITIES

Research suggests that facilitating a professional learning community contributes to teachers' pedagogical skills, subsequently influencing student learning (Gray, 2011). Similarly, Vesico, Ross, and Adam's (2008) review pointed out that well-developed professional learning communities have a positive impact on teaching practices and student learning. These authors also documented the positive impact of learning communities on teacher commitment, instructional practices, and engagement in school improvement. This is supported by studies indicating positive correlations between teachers' collegial learning and students' engagement and learning (e.g., Lee, Zhang, & Yin, 2011). Rosenholtz (1989) found that "developing" schools—those characterized by teachers learning from each other through a collective enterprise—are more effective than "stuck" schools, which lack such webs of interactions and therefore face more difficulties in implementing changes.

Unsurprisingly, in light of the accumulating body of evidence supporting their benefits, professional learning communities have become a major reform strategy in the new millennium to support teachers in meeting increased policy demands for high-stakes standardized testing and data-monitoring accountability (Gray & Summers, 2015). Efforts have been made to transform the mechanistic perspective into a more collaborative learning perspective in which teachers learn together and coordinate their efforts toward improved student learning (e.g., Drago-Severson, Roy, & Frank, 2014; Schechter, 2010; Steyn, 2013; Trust & Horrocks, 2017; Wake,

Swan, & Foster, 2016). Nevertheless, schools continue to struggle in implementing and especially in sustaining such collegial structures in the complex context of educational systems. Despite these efforts to bring collaborative learning to the forefront of school change discourse, teachers are still learning primarily from individual and isolated experiences rather than with and from their peers.

Another possible challenge to the implementation of professional learning communities is the danger that some learning communities can themselves perpetuate practitioners' skepticism toward any kind of communal learning. For example, the social arrangements wherein teachers share and create knowledge are often fraught with competition for professional legitimacy and political power, often inhibiting authentic interactions. Because legitimacy is conferred by community members rather than given automatically to individuals or a group, teachers may become reluctant to inquire into their own practices because of the possibly loose connections between their actions and the results ("Those outcomes could have occurred because of mere coincidence or luck and not directly because of my professional actions"). Thus, learning in the communal arena about the details of one's educational work can induce fear and vulnerability about possible harm to one's perceived professional legitimacy (Schechter, 2012).

Furthermore, time is perhaps the most salient issue influencing productive collegial interactions (Collinson & Cook, 2007), but in light of teachers' heavy workloads, sufficient time allocations are often lacking in schools. As a result, the supposed professional learning interactions frequently become mere updating mechanisms. Administrators tend to colonize the blocks of time allocated for collaborative learning and use them to advance their administrative agenda instead of focusing on instructional practices (Giles & Hargreaves, 2006; Park & So, 2014). In addition, there is a tendency to transform the professional learning model into a type of routine and everyday phenomenon, where any kind of encounter with an educational goal is mistakenly defined as a professional learning community (DuFour et al., 2006). Alternatively, from a change perspective, learning communities tend to isolate themselves, thereby blocking significant changes at the organizational level (Stoll & Louis, 2007). For example, teachers may meet together with their grade-level coordinator or their subject coordinator, but any collective learning achieved via such interactions may remain inaccessible to colleagues outside that group who might also find this content to be relevant to their work.

Professional learning communities are extremely difficult to embed into some existing school cultures, especially those upholding a primary focus on test scores and improving low academic achievements. Essentially, the professional learning process in such school cultures will likely be relegated to identifying and fixing only problems related to high-stakes standards. By and large, such learning communities will most often analyze school data in terms of "where we missed the mark"—where students lost points on state exams, how many students did not meet expectations, which subject areas showed the lowest scores, and so on. In this sense, reviewing failures and potential threats is most likely to perpetuate defensive group dynamics in which members fail to express and test their assumptions and refrain from authentic communication that may involve tension in the presence of their colleagues or supervisors.

In sum, the professional learning community framework is seldom translated effectively into a sustainable school reality that can serve as a viable tool for continuous school improvement and turnaround efforts over time. This leaves teachers and principals in need of more practical theories and guidance in order to effectively introduce and sustain more active and valuable communal learning in schools (Fullan, 2016; Schechter, 2012). Thus, although research has recognized the potential contribution of the professional learning community, uncertainty remains about its real-time development and sustainability within schools, especially in today's era of accountability and high-stakes standards (e.g., Hord, 2016). Can the professional learning community become more than a buzzword that superficially marks cutting-edge school leadership? Can we think about ways to design professional learning experiences for teachers that will have a direct impact on their practice and on outcomes for students? The aim of the current book is to transform the challenging implementation of learning communities into a more practical and achievable process for teachers, for building-level leaders, and for principals, based on their own strengths and professional expertise.

Specifically, as outlined step by step throughout the upcoming chapters, this book proposes that a practical and achievable bottom-up collective inquiry process should not only focus on the many problems facing teachers and school leaders but should also integrate the many successes that school professionals have achieved—their wisdoms of everyday practice—which generally go unnoticed and unanalyzed. Before presenting comprehensive details, vignettes, testimonies, and documents to help guide and inspire schools as they embark on their journey toward implementing effective professional learning communities, the next chapter takes a deeper look at the three main foundations of this approach—learning collectively, learning from problems, and learning from successes. These three foundations are the essential building blocks needed to shift schools toward operative, sustainable collaborative learning communities.

CHAPTER 2

How to Learn Collectively

Gleaning Wisdom From Professionals' Problems and Successes

> Collective learning benefits everyone involved. Just as I can give something to the process, I can gain from it. We should have the capacity to create a good atmosphere of respect and collaboration, reduce competition, and direct everyone toward learning together.
>
> —a high school teacher

> Today, we consciously include regular hours for the staff to get together and learn from our experiences. I set a permanent timeframe in which teachers get together, sharing their thoughts and knowledge, reflecting on how they adapt the curriculum to diverse students, and taking collaborative responsibility.
>
> —a high school principal

As crucial background for any school's attempt to pursue professional learning communities as a built-in vehicle for continually achieving further school improvement over time, the current chapter discusses the three rudiments underlying this approach: learning collectively, learning from problems, and learning from successes. This chapter begins by briefly reviewing collective retrospective learning in schools and then proceeds to explore the widespread human predisposition to learn from problems and failures, pinpointing both the opportunities afforded by this form of learning as well as the obstacles it poses. This chapter then expands on the limitations and the potential benefits of learning from educators' successful practices and positive experiences—which will be developed and exemplified in detail in the ensuing chapters.

LEARNING COLLECTIVELY AND RETROSPECTIVELY

Collective learning from professional practices is considered an important pedagogical framework for developing teachers' capacities to meet the growing challenges in today's schoolwork. This *collaborative learning* or *collective learning* framework represents a shift in emphasis from teachers' teaching to the notion of teachers themselves as learners (Le Cornu & Ewing, 2008; Michalsky & Schechter, 2013). Thus, collective processes that encourage teachers to reflect on their professional results and learn from them have enjoyed widespread application in teachers' professional development around the world (e.g., Edwards & Hammer, 2006; Schechter & Michalsky, 2014). This shift toward collective learning resonates with Dewey's argument that "we do not learn from experience. . . . We learn from [collectively] reflecting on our experiences" (1933, p. 78).

Collective retrospective learning requires a process of *reconstruction* wherein learners systematically analyze their behaviors that previously led to performance outcomes. Practitioners can generate and reorganize professional knowledge through their ongoing discussion of past experiences. Through a process of "reflection-on-action" (Schon, 1983), practitioners deliberately reflect on specific incidents they experienced as well as on the effects of their actions on their environments. This "reflection–conversation" process (Grimmett, 1988) creates a dialogue between the cognitive frameworks constructed by practitioners based on information in their practice setting and their own existing mental frameworks (Schechter, 2012).

Collective retrospective reviews are forums in which members of an organization can make sense out of their past experiences within their own specific context. Through "shared narration," the organization's members recount past experiences and collectively discuss them to construct the reality of that organization (Brown & Duguid, 1996). When intentionally designed, this sensemaking yielded by collective retrospective reviews should create what Daft and Weick (1984) referred to as "interpretation systems." Thus, in schools, the collective analysis of past experiences leads practitioners not only to a new understanding of practical situations but also to an exploration of preconceived tacit assumptions about teaching. Consequently, learning from past experiences leads to better self-understanding, better understanding of the teaching profession, and better integration between the two. These inter-negotiations of beliefs and opinions evaluate multiple perspectives, check errors, and consequently stimulate new insights, leading Huber (1996) to claim that collective retrospective reviews can be an important organizational mechanism for promoting double-loop learning. *Double-loop learning* does not rely only on instrumental (*single-loop*) learning, which leaves an organization's existing values and norms unexamined but rather adds inquiry into underlying assumptions and strategies. Reflective conversations with past experiences are thus the building blocks of professional development. They shape, construct, and reconstruct the cognitive professional habits of practitioners in educational enterprises (Schechter, 2010, 2011c, 2012).

Collective retrospective learning is of special relevance to school communities, in order to enable knowledge—whether enacted formally or informally, deliberately or unintentionally—to be constructed through collective interpretation of experiences shared among school members (Louis, 2006). Growing evidence suggests that extensive use of collective learning mechanisms related to curriculum and instruction promotes greater teacher commitment and student engagement in school practices. *Collective learning mechanisms* in schools may include teacher teams working together on ways to improve curriculum and instruction, staff meetings held to discuss school goals, teachers working in dyads or small groups to plan educational activities, or subject-matter teachers collaborating to adapt curricula to diverse students' needs. In studies of schools at all levels, ranging from primary to secondary (Schechter, 2008a; Schechter & Atarchi, 2014), collective learning mechanisms have been shown to positively correlate both with teachers' sense of collective efficacy and with teachers' commitment to their school. Moreover, studies demonstrated that collective learning enhanced teachers' sense of pedagogical competence and promoted teachers' utilization of inquiry-based instructional techniques. Similarly, collegial learning has been shown to be effective in increasing teachers' inquiry into instructional materials and practices within the school, which, in turn, facilitated teachers' use of innovative pedagogical methods (e.g., De Neve, Devos, & Tuytens, 2015; Printy, 2008).

What are the resources and experiences necessary for productive collective learning? How can educators develop their capacity to deliberate productively on professional experiences and events? Two main approaches are explored next: learning from problems and learning from successes.

LEARNING FROM PROBLEMS

> Learning from success is something that creates euphoria; there is that sense of "We did it!" so we think it will keep happening like that. When we teachers succeed, we don't force ourselves to go into all the details and learn from it. Deep and significant learning can come only from problems. The more traumatic the problem, the more it knocks you to the ground, the more you learn, deep down.
>
> —a high school math coordinator

> I think that we need to look for the things that aren't succeeding, and to see those problems as challenging us to think and act differently. Problematic aspects bring us toward new thinking. When we succeed, great, wonderful—all we need to do is think about how to improve or add to it. But when we fail, we have a problem, and we need to learn and to change things.
>
> —a middle school teacher

> Learning from failures is much more interesting. When I was in the United States on a study visit, I wanted to see high schools that are facing difficulties. I wanted to figure out why they weren't succeeding so as to learn how not to repeat others' mistakes. Now, here, we are learning from others' problematic experiences.
>
> —a high school principal

Learning from problems, which involves drawing lessons from past problematic events, is a learning method used widely in a variety of fields (Barber, King, & Buchanan, 2015; Elder, 2015). The interrelationship between problems and learning is rooted in diverse sources, especially in those that view learning as a process of problem solving. To illustrate, Dewey (1933, pp. 100–101) asserted that the human cognitive operation of *reflection* consistently arises from states of difficulty, perplexity, or uncertainty, which call for a resolution: "The function of reflective thought is, therefore, to transform a situation in which there is experienced obscurity, doubt, conflict, disturbance of some sort, into a situation that is clear, coherent, settled, harmonious." Dewey's moral philosophy formulated methods for dealing with the problematic situations within human experiences and conditions (Gouinlock, 1992), which arise when individuals' ongoing activity is impeded or disrupted. According to this view, thinking about problems as a source of reflection and discovery opens a space for new knowledge, as relevant information comes to light and as new questions arise.

This notion of *problems as catalysts* for dynamic individual and organizational learning and growth needs to be distinguished from the notion of a *problem of practice*. In a problem of practice, a teacher problematizes a classroom event in order to develop reflective capacity as a particular habit of mind that enables more complex examination of teaching practices (Schechter, 2011c, 2012). Nonetheless, teachers may conceptualize a situation as a problem based on its perceived difficulty level or negative outcomes, even when the incident itself might be judged as a successful teaching event.

Explicit claims have been made in the fields of social psychology and organizational behavior asserting that past failed events and problematic experiences are an essential prerequisite for learning (Ellis & Davidi, 2005). According to Dodgson (1993), psychological theories on learning perceive conflict as a necessary condition for triggering a learning process. Kolb (1984) also argued that perceived discomfort and perplexity serve as a stimulus for growth. This perspective was also evident in Argyris and Schon's (1996) definition of *organizational learning* as a mechanism of detecting and correcting errors. Feldman (1989), too, considered the noticing of errors to be necessary for learning.

Indeed, people do tend to engage in conscious learning when they are frustrated by failures and disruptions. In other words, when individuals encounter problems, obstructions, or unexpected malfunctions, they need to generate various hypotheses to explain what happened and to think about how to solve the negative consequences. In this way, unpleasant and undesirable events serve as a trigger for conscious *post-action reviews*—which may include attention, awareness, reflection, and hypothesis testing—and thereby stimulate a process of sensemaking (Mahenswaran & Chaiken, 1991). Times of crisis, in this regard, can be seen as the ultimate motivator for human learning. At the organizational level, this view upholds that organizations' learning is initiated in response to the perception of problems. Put differently, learning is triggered when performance level deteriorates or an upcoming breakdown is perceived. Therefore, social psychologists and organizational behaviorists have acknowledged that the predominant productive trigger for reflection and change should be the incorporation of learning from past problems into organizational practices (Schechter, 2011b).

In line with other disciplines of inquiry, in the education realm, the examination of past events (*retrospective reviews*) has been closely associated with tackling problems in a collaborative forum. The ability for a group to reconstruct and reorganize the professional knowledge generated by past experiences has been directly linked with that group's capacity to confront problems and develop solutions (Marks & Louis, 1999). Moreover, learning in the form of communal deliberations—the collective rehearsal of various competing possible lines of action—has been perceived as "the method by which most everyday practical problems get solved" (Schwab, 1978, p. 43). Likewise, Walker (1990) emphasized practical problems as the seed for initiating deliberative processes, and Dillon (1994) suggested that teachers should deliberate in order to decide how best to solve the problematic circumstance.

Unsurprisingly, this approach is reflected in the clear problem-focused slant upheld by the available literature on school administration, which accentuates learning as centered on collectively solving problems to eliminate undesirable conditions. Taking this perspective, the conscious collective attempt to identify and reframe problems is an important prerequisite for effective school administration (Schechter, 2011b). Consequently, overall, learning in schools has been conditioned toward school-related experiences and circumstances that have gone wrong, which are approached and deliberated from a problem-solving orientation.

Numerous scholars have emphasized the virtue of examining problems to promote learning. Sitkin (1996) argued that problems stimulate a high willingness to consider alternatives and to critique traditional working patterns. Thus, problems stimulate an "unfreezing" process (Schein, 1992) necessary for initiating learning—an opening up to new possibilities. There is also evidence suggesting that information reflecting problems is more salient to the performer than information indicating success. A problem—namely performance below aspiration level—signals unequivocally and explicitly that one's results demand cognitive exploration and change (Lant & Mezias, 1992). This corresponds to Lounammaa and March's (1987) assertion that practitioners treat "performance improvements as confounded but treat performance decrements as containing information" (p. 116). In view of these tendencies, in a trial-and-error learning process, change in behavior is more likely when performance is below aspiration level. Overall, according to Bubsy (1999), the collective sensemaking process in organizations holds a number of functions based on reflections about the problems encountered: (1) to explore why and how things went wrong; (2) to formulate remedies; (3) to enrich communal knowledge; and (4) to provide a platform for interpretations of organizational history in a more open and secure space, which is less possible in the daily course of work.

Although failures and problems represent different circumstances, they both stimulate a conscious search for meaning and clearly signify that learning should take place. Thus, scholars have advanced the notions of problem finding and problem solving as a proactive, analytical, and strategic process, thereby couching problem-based learning as a domain for ongoing and progressive inquiry (Schechter, 2011b; Sroufe & Ramos, 2015). As described above, problems and failures can stimulate a critique of traditional working patterns, generating an unfreezing process in which organization members are able to perceive the need for change despite their tendency to maintain the status quo—a process necessary for initiating organizational change (Schein, 1992).

However, reviewing problems can also be associated with responses of denial and avoidance. Practitioners involved in reviewing failures may potentially experience a sense of threat, which tends to perpetuate the same defensive dynamics that may have contributed to the failure in the first place, hence restricting authentic inquiry and possible change (Slavich & Zimbardo, 2012). When attending collective forums, learning is often characterized by defensive exchanges, where members fail to express and test their assumptions and refrain from communication that may involve tension (Argyris & Schon, 1996). These "learning disabilities" (Senge, 2006) or "dysfunctional learning habits" (Louis, 2006) function "in a self-maintaining, self-reinforcing pattern that is anti-learning and noncorrective" (Argyris, 1993, p. 243). In addition, ongoing and persistent learning from failures can produce instability in beliefs and disagreements among peers about preferences and actions, both of which interfere with efforts to generate collective learning from past professional experiences.

In sum, problems and failures can challenge practitioners to question the status quo and seek alternative courses of action as effective triggers for learning, which can lead to double-loop learning that enables questioning of deep-rooted assumptions and norms behind actions. Consequently, failures may be perceived as the ultimate teacher (Schechter, 2011b). However, because of the potential sense of threat inherent in acknowledging problems or failures, practitioners often become entrenched in denial and avoidance, which can maintain the problematic status quo. In other words, problems and failures, under various school circumstances such as the threat of being shut down because the school is not meeting its annual development criteria, may not provide a database that is conducive to collective learning (Ellis & Davidi, 2005; Schechter, 2010). Thus, in schools, the potential threat for teachers involved in reviewing problems and failures tends to perpetuate the same defensive dynamics that may have contributed to the problem/failure in the first place, thereby restricting authentic inquiry into teachers' wisdom of practice. Learning from successes may pose an alternative, as seen next.

LEARNING FROM SUCCESSES

When you ask, "Where do you see success?" you deconstruct it so that it becomes a conscious process. In my opinion, when describing a success, we can't just show what happened—a mere description of the successful event doesn't do any good. We need to really reflect on what we learned and how it contributed to our knowledge; for example, maybe it strengthened something that we are already doing. Conceptualizing our successful experiences is very demanding, although this is a critical stage for the faculty in becoming a learning group. We need to be sure that we don't just put successes away into our "mental safes." It is a wake-up call for us.

—an elementary school principal

We are accustomed to learning from failures—how to detect and correct undesirable results. Now we need to turn 180 degrees around in our terminology and focus on our successes, something we seldom pay attention to. Our terminology needs to be changed.

—a high school teacher

Learning from problems is easy—we learn what not to do. Learning from success, however, is much more complicated because we learn what we need to do and how to make the relevant adaptations to the learner.

—an elementary school teacher

Growing dissatisfaction with the social, physical, and linguistic architecture of schoolwork calls for the introduction of new ways, opportunities, and spaces for all school stakeholders to carry out dialogue and cooperate (Mulford & Silins, 2011; Schechter, 2013). As described above, collaborative learning processes in schools, which take place by means of group reflection, have generally been associated with problem finding and problem solving and therefore have been selectively inattentive to school successes. Yet, an alternative strategy for inquiring into the professional wisdom of school members is through collective learning from success, which shifts the group's selective focus of learning from problems and failures to a selective focus on previously unexplored successful practices. This type of success-based learning group—the main focus of the current book—deliberately and collaboratively works to uncover the tacit wisdom (*actionable knowledge*, according to Argyris, 1993) that made these successes possible. *Professional wisdom* is comprised of experience, knowledge, and good judgment, which reflect what actually works in practice (Argyris & Schon, 1996). *Wisdom*, as an action-oriented concept, is the ability to best use knowledge and experience for exercising good judgment when implementing strategies and achieving desired goals (Bierly, Kessler, & Christensen, 2000). Hence, social learning arrangements for conscious reflection on successful practices can nurture the gradual emergence of professional knowledge (Schechter, Sykes, & Rosenfeld, 2004, 2008).

The focus on learning from successes coincides with *positive psychology* (Seligman & Csikszentmihalyi, 2000), a perspective exploring the nature of effectively functioning individuals or organizations undergoing a continuous learning process (Hoy & Tarter, 2011). Framing positive aspects of school practices as important learning opportunities also has philosophical grounding in the literature on appreciative inquiry (Coperrider, Sorensen, & Whitney, 2000; Whitney & Fredrickson, 2015) and on positive organizational scholarship (Cameron, Dutton, & Quinn, 2003; Nilsson, 2015). Rather than focusing on deficit-based practices, these approaches give prominence to discovering what works well and how successes can generate a more positive course of human and organizational welfare. Thus, these approaches underscore the positive strengths of organizational members and how these strengths can support team members.

Learning from success primarily focuses on the collective learning endeavor, investigating the situations that an organization cherishes as meaningful, successful, and important, while extracting from them various lessons for the future and steps aimed at change (see Chapter 4 for the learning-from-success journey). Learning from success is aimed at uncovering organization members' knowledge that has contributed to the success of past actions while capturing the specific practices performed along the way. The goal of learning from success is to create a learning community that investigates its own beneficial actions, a community that focuses on discovering team members' professional wisdom and identifying action-oriented knowledge.

Several major assumptions underlie the notion of collaborative learning from success in the education domain. These may include the following postulations (Schechter et al., 2008):

1. The expertise of teachers in schools is a rich, barely tapped resource.

2. Due to systemic bias toward learning from difficulties or problems in schools, successes have rarely been the object of deliberate learning.

3. For the expertise that underlies success to be tapped, it must undergo a collective learning process through which individuals' knowledge is transformed into organizational knowledge, thereby assisting school faculty members in explicitly exploring their wisdom of practice.

Thus, at its core, collective learning from success in schools focuses on identifying the tacit knowledge that is inherent in past successes and transforming it into explicit knowledge, expressed in *actionable language*, for future use. The assumption is that the use of activities that contributed to success in the past can serve as a basis for the identification of *action principles* that contribute to success in the future. Metaphorically, just as archeology is a platform for the use of reconstructed artifacts in order to promote understanding and knowledge, the reconstruction of success stories in human services creates an opportunity to use the resulting knowledge to sketch the contours of what should be done (Rosenfeld et al., 1995). Action principles derived from deliberate collaborative inquiry into past successes may be used to attain desired outcomes in the future.

In particular, in retrospective learning from successful practices, practitioners identify their professional successes and coordinate structured group inquiries into the actions that contributed to these successes. In other words, educators reflect upon their own past school successes, discovering and explicating the knowledge that contributed to those successes and formulating them in actionable terms as a basis for their dissemination. Learning from success aims to reveal the hidden knowledge that contributed to those earlier successful practices and to capture the specific actions that were taken along the path to success. Therefore, persistence in viewing the success from the action perspective is essential to enable teachers to reconnect with what they did that worked (Schechter et al., 2004, 2008).

CHALLENGING ASPECTS OF LEARNING FROM SUCCESS

While the professional literature has alluded to learning from success in organizations, including schools, it has focused mainly on the problematic dynamics that may ensue. Researchers have suggested several possible problems or risks that collective learning from success could elicit. For example, learning from success may

(a) lead to actions that preserve the status quo and avoid risk taking (Ellis, Mendel, & Nir, 2006);

(b) induce overconfidence and self-assurance in routines that were proven successful in the past (Gino & Pisano, 2011);

(c) strengthen organizations' homogeneity, where maintenance of the same historical operating procedures and the same personnel impedes experimentation with organizational routines (Madsen & Desai, 2010; Sitkin, 1996);

(d) only rarely stimulate a conscious search for meaning (*failure to ask why* syndrome) and may be processed, if at all, by "automatic pilot" (Ellis & Davidi, 2005);

(e) produce only first-order learning, reducing the likelihood that organizations will respond to environmental change with transformational change (Lundin, Öberg, & Josefsson, 2015; Virany, Tushman, & Romanelli, 1996);

(f) cause strategic inertia, inattentiveness, and isolation if implemented for long periods, thus increasing the probability of future problems (Baumard & Starbuck, 2005); or

(g) provide little attention to the role that environmental factors and random events may have played, focusing much more on current models or strategies (Gino & Pisano, 2011).

Overall, such unwanted problematic dynamics can be articulated in the following way. Collaborative learning from successes may provide collective assurances to certain professional practices, legitimizing them as desirable within the particular school context. Taking this perspective, collective learning from successful practices will be less focused on generating new strategies through flexibility and discovery processes and, instead, will be more focused on refining the efficiency of familiar strategies already deemed appropriate (March, 1996). In other words, by exploiting routines that proved successful in the past, there is a danger that learners will be less likely to seek out or pay attention to new and alternative information that might indicate a need to change routines (Schechter, 2010).

Successful cases are difficult to analyze for several reasons. First, with regard to teachers' professional wisdom in particular, a disadvantage of collective learning from successes may be that "success" is a tricky and messy thing to document and learn about. When focusing on collective learning from successful practices, it is well known that educators do not necessarily share the same beliefs and values about what counts as success. As a result, one teacher's perceived success may be another's perceived problem. This complexity is deepened because success is always relative to particular organizational goals. Inasmuch as teachers must address multiple goals simultaneously, the achievement of some goals is always at the expense of others (Schechter, 2012).

Second, success at the schoolwide performance level is seldom direct or intentional. As Weick (1982) describes in his "loose coupling" theory, to meet performance goals, schools often draw on capacities that have developed via tangential, even irrelevant functions of their organization. Therefore, when discussing and analyzing successes, teachers are able to point out only proximal, intentional factors that appeared to have contributed to successes but often remain unable to identify the myriad underlying capacities that established the conditions for the possibility of recent success. In this sense, many of the success stories in schools that result from combinations of situational and organizational factors are not known to the individual classroom teacher. Put differently, the loosely coupled structure of schools—with teachers usually operating in isolation—withholds teachers' ability to apply new information regarding successful core instructional processes across classrooms (Halverson, Grigg, Prichett, & Thomas, 2005; Schechter, 2011b).

Third, people involved in complex practices are often unable to recall and reconstruct the concrete actions that led to successful outcomes. This may pose a problem because the point of collective analysis is to communicate the salient, critical factors of practice that led to success. When learners are unaware of the key contributors to their successful practices, some evidence must be provided to make sure that the analyzed success stories accurately reflect not only the positive capacity building but also the negative practices that led up to the successful outcomes: These may include false starts, early failures, misdirection, and multiple initiatives that eventually led to the successful results.

Fourth, the dynamics of sharing a success story may be inherently complex. Analysis of teachers' reported successes in the communal arena may induce feelings of fear and vulnerability about one's own professional legitimacy in the eyes of peers and supervisors. Professional legitimacy is tightly linked to practitioners' expectations regarding their colleagues' expertise and knowledge (Beaulieu, Roy, & Pasquero, 2002). Therefore, by publicly displaying what one perceives as a success, one runs the risk of not having this definition of success fully recognized by the collective, which could potentially reshape perceptions of one's professional legitimacy. Thus, the collective learning process from successful practices may be experienced by teachers as a threat to their professional recognition by their colleagues.

BENEFITS OF LEARNING FROM SUCCESS

Without denying the validity of the above claims, the predominant bias in the literature against learning from success too often prevents professionals from gaining from the wealth of learning opportunities embedded in their own practices. In this vein, it is important to discuss considerations on the benefits of collective learning from success. Collaborative learning from success can

1. reduce defensiveness and enhance motivation,

2. generate transformation,

3. enhance reflection on effective practices,

4. create positive organizational memory, and

5. generate a commitment to and an investment in learning among diverse members of a school community.

These benefits are elaborated next, to map out some of the important answers to the question, "Why should our school initiate collective learning-from-success processes?"

Learning From Success Can Reduce Defensiveness and Enhance Motivation

A continuous process of inquiry into successful events should not occur under external pressure (as is often the case for problematic and failed events) but rather as a result of voluntary intrinsic interest in initiating and participating in a learning process. Hence, practitioners are more inclined to investigate successful events as a source of comfort and motivation instead of immediately delving into the emotional and cognitive stress involved in discussing failed events. Moreover, the pressure associated with reviewing failed events directs cognitive attention toward seeking immediate causes, whereas the review of successful events allows for a more open, creative, and reflective approach during which practitioners can let down some of their defensiveness and open themselves up to exploring and questioning themselves and others. Whereas failures trigger an immediate search for causes in order to justify them, successes encourage a more systematic and less biased analysis of learners' mental models (Ellis & Davidi, 2005).

Another benefit of the success-based approach can be found in Sitkin's (1996) argument that success enhances confidence and persistence and stimulates a coordinated pursuit to achieve common goals. After learning that a specific action has been successful, practitioners are more confident in their competence and achievements and are more motivated and satisfied (Schechter et al., 2008). In this way, initiating an early process of learning from successes tends to become a self-fulfilling prophecy, which translates into a greater probability of learning from subsequent success (Gino & Pisano, 2011). Identification of success in important areas of activity that previously elicited a great degree of frustration and helplessness revitalizes investment and motivation in these areas.

While memories based on failed experiences may impede new learning efforts, which can be fatal to any collective retrospective learning experience (Lant & Mezias, 1992), positive shared memories may reduce defensiveness, creating a sense of openness to and desire for future learning. In other words, organizations that accumulate enough shared experiences of learning from success are better equipped to collectively tackle, solve, and learn from organizational failures. Thus, although learning from success has been criticized as the enemy of experimentation and innovation (Levitt & March, 1996), the deliberate choice to learn from successful practices can serve as a springboard for nurturing productive inquiry into professional wisdom.

Learning From Success Can Generate Transformation

Learning from success is most meaningful when the successes reflected upon are precisely those in which there is an element of surprise or dissonance from mainstream practices. Just as learning from failure can lead to participants' questioning of accepted practices, so can learning from success lead to participants' inquiry into tacit assumptions by focusing on those practices that are distinctly different and more successful than accepted ones. The dissonance experienced, in this case, however, is the successful event rather than the failed one (Rosenfeld, 1997). The surprise emanates from engagement in revisiting, decoding, and then explicating the many unnoticed actions that made success possible in the first place (Rosenfeld & Sykes, 1998; Schechter, 2011b) and in tracing its unintended expanding circles of impact.

Furthermore, learning from success may offer a ray of optimism in the face of pessimism and helplessness. In many organizational contexts, educators have come to accept their education system's failure to achieve its desired outcomes as inevitable. Put differently, practitioners and schools often feel weak and powerless about their probability of achieving meaningful positive results in the face of longstanding, intractable social gaps and near-impossible expectations from parents, the media, and supervisors. When this pessimism becomes rooted in the school's culture, its mainstream teaching practices can become oriented toward acceptance of failure. In such contexts, such as urban schools that are labeled *low-performing*, it is precisely the analysis of successful stories by practitioners that actually offers potential for transformation. Under such circumstances, learning from successful events can serve as a trigger for stimulating conscious reflection both as pertaining to underlying assumptions and as pertaining to possible actions that could create unexpected positive results (Schechter et al., 2008).

Specifically, collective learning from success can transform school staff's belief in the school's effectiveness as a whole. Collaborative explication of the detailed actions that led to past successful practices can enhance the school faculty members' collective efficacy with regard to the whole group's possible positive impact on future student achievement. In other words, the focus on successes during collective learning can bring to light positive recognition of underlying faculty expertise, fostering a shared belief in the capacity of the school and its staff to succeed in their tasks and to learn from their experiences. Thus, learning from success reinforces the learning competence of practitioners (e.g., teachers, principals) and instills in them appreciation, respect, and even wonder at the value of their own accomplishments, strengthening a positive-reinforcement feedback cycle (Schechter et al., 2008). In this way, detailed collaborative learning about past successful actions not only enhances learners' collective efficacy with regard to the group's capacity to learn from their own professional practices in that particular challenging school context but also fosters their belief that the group can significantly promote students' well-being and academic achievements.

Learning From Success Can Enhance Reflection on Effective Practices

Learning from success starts by identifying instances in professional life in which desired outcomes were achieved, particularly when those outcomes were the product of effective professional action. Namely, the focus of inquiry is twofold: on desired outcomes and on what was done in the past to achieve them. In contrast to evaluating failures and near-failures in order to prevent them from future occurrence (a classical approach of risk administration), the goal of learning from success is to perpetuate and reinforce these successes—a classic quality improvement approach. By encouraging conscious explanations about successful events, the collective learning-from-success process stimulates additional hypotheses concerning the performance. This provides additional valid information concerning the connections between teachers' actions and consequences at a variety of levels in the school—within the student, between the teacher and student, between peers in the classroom, within the grade or subject matter, in relation to parents, and so forth. Clearer action–consequence connections facilitate and enhance more accurate feedback, which is greatly needed in educational settings, especially in today's climate of accountability policies and high-stakes standards. When practicing learning from success, practitioners become aware of their own expertise and the expertise of others, and they begin to develop a refined awareness of the detailed ways in which such expertise finds expression in their practice (Rosenfeld & Sykes, 1998). Thus, the key to learning from success is selective attention that is deliberately focused on successes in order to uncover the wisdom that made them possible.

Learning From Success Can Create Positive Organizational Memory

Collective learning about professional successes acknowledges that a web of professional expertise exists within the group, which, in turn, can develop a tradition of contributing to the shared knowledge base. Through analyzing professional successes, the individual's pedagogical expertise is transferred into a shared knowledge base for the benefit of all faculty members. Analyzing successful practices serves as a database from which practitioners can draw professional knowledge relevant to their work. As a consequence, the deliberate analysis of successful practices in the collective arena can develop an interactive positive "memory" that contains teaching practices, resource room materials, documents, stories, artifacts, and more. This organizational "memory" is distinct and more developed than individual memory because it combines the ongoing interrelated activities, processes, and methods of multiple staff members (Kruse, 2003; Schechter, 2008a). Interestingly, this learning mechanism can serve as the school's "brain" by collecting information from individual teachers and combining it into a common shared knowledge. The process of learning from success, then, encodes individual pedagogical practices into a collective professional mind that is distinct from the individual mind and clearly surpasses it.

Learning From Success Can Generate a Commitment to and an Investment in Learning Among Diverse Members of the School Community

The search for and focus on successes of school members frequently calls attention to a range of positive processes that had previously gone relatively unnoticed. This act of learning, which essentially entails "search and reflection," demands cooperation among a variety of stakeholders both at the school level (teachers, nonteaching staff, students, and parents) and outside the school (superintendents, community leaders, district leaders, policymakers). Inevitably, learning that is based on collectively analyzing the path to professional success creates an atmosphere of reciprocity, which removes the hierarchal types of barriers that tend to bar joint organizational learning ventures. The school learning process becomes leverage for the disseminators and the initiators of new knowledge-based work methods both within and outside the school (Sabah & Rosenfeld, 2001). In this way, recognizing and learning from these activities awakens a sense of professional pride and competence.

In sum, the following picture emerges from the above exploration of the advantages and limitations of collective learning from either problems or successes. Problems and failures that challenge practitioners to question the status quo and seek alternative courses of action are the most common triggers to learning. However, because of the potential threat involved in acknowledging problems or failures, such opportunities to learn are frequently missed, as practitioners become entrenched in denial and avoidance that maintain a problematic status quo. In other words, problems and failures do not necessarily provide a database conducive to learning. Successes, though, especially in organizational contexts in which the achievement of successful outcomes is the exception rather than the rule, are opportunities for transformational learning (Schechter, 2011b; Schechter et al., 2008). Learning from successful practices can become a core collaborative inquiry process that allows for the reconceptualization and emergence of professional wisdom within diverse contexts and policies. Now that this chapter has explored the main building blocks underlying collective learning, not only from problems but also from successes, the upcoming chapter examines how actual practitioners perceive such attempts to learn collaboratively from their own wisdoms of practice in schools.

CHAPTER 3

Juggling Our Mindsets

Educators' Perceptions of Collective Learning From Success

> In schools, we often target failure and we try to design curriculum, programs, and activities around how to overcome our students' shortcomings rather than learning from what they are doing well.
>
> —a high school teacher

> Unfortunately, the Ministry of Education acts out of a sense of failure and fear because of the poor results of our students. There is no deep learning about why we do well in times of success.
>
> —a middle school principal

> We need to learn from our successes, not out of competitiveness or jealousy, but rather out of a generous approach that facilitates the staff's learning. Obviously, there should be preparation beforehand, and the staff should be part of it so that they feel there's joint learning without any labeling of a "good" or "bad" teacher.
>
> —an elementary school teacher

Mindscapes are like road maps that provide rules, images, and principles for school practitioners; they define what teaching, learning, and school leadership are and how their practice should unfold at the micro and macro levels

(Sergiovanni, 2005). Mindscapes function as personal theories that help practitioners navigate in an uncertain and complex educational context. Exploring practitioners' different mindscapes can provide a broader view of the collective learning-from-success process in the context of the educational system, with implications for its potential implementation and maintenance. Thus, this chapter aims not only to give voice to teachers' perceptions about their schools' efforts to learn from success but also to explore the conditions necessary for igniting such collective learning processes in school systems.

This chapter presents research (derived in part from Schechter, 2015) that explored teachers' mindscapes concerning collective learning from success, specifically the determinants for its successful implementation in the school system. Participants were 78 teachers (72 women, six men; 39 in elementary schools, 30 in middle schools, nine in high schools), mainly from urban school settings, teaching diverse subject matters and serving in various organizational roles. Although it was not possible to select a random sample of teachers, participants worked in public elementary, middle, and high schools, representing the entire socioeconomic range. Data were collected via face-to-face semi-structured interviews designed to explore participants' personal perspectives (Marshall & Rossman, 2011). Using a semi-structured interview guide to collect data from all participants enabled exploration of participants' personal perspectives while interviewing the different individuals more systematically.

None of these participants had previously been exposed to the idea of collective learning from success, either in their formal education or throughout their professional development. Therefore, the interviewer stated the following at the beginning of each interview: "Learning from success is a group inquiry, which identifies and analyzes staff's and students' successes. Learning from success is a collective inquiry into the detailed actions that contributed to professional successes." This was followed by questions such as *What are your thoughts and feelings when relating the idea of collective learning from success to your work at school? Can you identify possible impediments to this collective learning process? Can you identify possible positive contributors to this collective learning process?*

What follows are the five major determinants regarded by teachers as important in facilitating collective learning from success: (1) the learning culture, (2) defining the term *success*, (3) a focus on tests and assessments, (4) leadership for learning, and (5) organizational resources.

1. THE LEARNING CULTURE

According to interviewed teachers, the school's learning culture is salient in fostering or inhibiting learning from success. The learning culture was mentioned as a major determinant to learning from success by 78.5% of the interviewed teachers. Within the learning culture, three major interconnected themes were described: relationships among the staff, a competitive atmosphere, and talk about levels of experience.

STAFF RELATIONSHIPS

Interviewees reported that the extent to which teachers can collaborate in their schools' collective processes of learning from success is inexorably linked to the existence of positive collegial relationships (e.g., openness, trust, and support) or to negative relationships (e.g., tensions, envy). Teachers believe that sharing their successes with other teachers—and the exposure involved in this process—requires a positive emotional climate and a sense of safety, respect, and support:

> In collective learning from success, there must be ground rules established in order for each person to be heard and respected based on what they bring to the table to share.
>
> —a middle school math teacher

> To produce the climate necessary for such a process to take place, the school first needs to create a work infrastructure that will allow for it—an atmosphere of sharing, understanding, and mutual respect and to adequately examine the staff members to see if they are even able to advance such a process productively. Personally, I'm still hesitant, unsure if we have stable ground to stand on that will allow such immense exposure to take place.
>
> —an elementary school homeroom teacher

> Most teachers want to work in an atmosphere of transparency, where their success receives recognition, where they feel that they have things to learn from others' success, working in an encouraging system that gives them credit. This makes for the creation of a safer and more enabling system for the teachers, which endows teachers with both the right and the duty to impact the school atmosphere and the professionalism of their peers on the staff.
>
> —a high school history teacher

The latter interview excerpt accentuates the importance of a generous learning culture where teaching staff members acknowledge each other's accomplishments as a factor enhancing learning from success. Several teachers also spoke about trust among staff members as another crucial factor for advancing learning from success:

> I think feeling trusting and comfortable with your colleagues is very helpful, so that you can share your success and somehow remove the threat that it might be used against you. This is very important.
>
> —a middle school science teacher

> With trust, you build respect, and with trust and respect, it is easier to collaborate and have some collective thoughts and ideas regarding our successes.
>
> —a middle school literature teacher

> First of all, you have to trust each other. There has to be that comfort level. . . . Teachers have to be able to trust that the people in the group will not say negative things about them, that they are there to help and support.
>
> —an elementary school English teacher

As seen, teachers expressed their need to have trust in the process of learning from success, allowing acceptance of diversity among teachers. In sum, teachers felt that for learning from success to be productive, the school staff must have positive relationships and the school environment must be sensed as safe. In contrast, a negative school atmosphere laden with tense or jealous interpersonal relationships may impede the learning-from-success process:

> Negatively, I can see teachers violating the norms of professional interaction; talking behind each other's backs, judging each other harshly, being negative about the whole process, and trying to sabotage the process so they can go back to being alone in their classroom.
>
> —a high school chemistry teacher

> In this school, there are quite a few intrigues, so reaching agreements here is nearly impossible. . . . Personally, I would be worried about the staff not agreeing to share or even listen when it comes to their successes. I can imagine a certain teacher telling about a successful experience, while the rest of the

THE COLLECTIVE WISDOM OF PRACTICE

teachers might be secretly resentful—asking themselves, *Why did that teacher succeed and I didn't?* . . . Another reason for my apprehension is the teachers' criticism: Let's say a certain teacher shares his experiences with the staff. The other staff members might find fault with his story or undermine his confidence, which will cause him to stop cooperating with the process.

—an elementary school pedagogical coordinator

If people will react aggressively to my success, I won't tell about such instances and I'll close up. This will cause other teachers to close up, too. But if people will know how to react, offering their negative comments in a constructive and caring way, in a mode that will contribute to their colleagues, that will bring about learning from success.

—an elementary school literature teacher

Thus, the interviewed teachers felt that any negative judgments and criticisms by peers during collective learning would be likely to have an inhibitory effect on the learning-from-success process. Teachers even expressed concern that learning from success might become a professional threat:

The teachers would need to see value in the practice and be told that they are not being evaluated or judged professionally during this process; that there would not be any negative impact on their employment status based on what happens during this collective learning process.

—a high school math teacher

Worries about the harmful use of shared knowledge by colleagues and lack of mutual respect may influence school culture negatively in cases where teachers might be risking their social, professional, or occupational status by sharing their success stories. In such cases, teachers asserted that the potential benefits from learning from success would not be worth the risks involved.

AN ATMOSPHERE OF COMPETITION

Strong competitiveness was reported to be a major obstacle to productive learning from success because it may lead to a school learning environment where the success of the few is seen as more important than the success of teams or of the whole organization. A competitive atmosphere can cause tensions, jealousy, and a negative ambience, as described by the following elementary school teachers:

It can create a kind of competitiveness. Like, what are you saying, that you're better than I am? You did it and I couldn't, so what does that mean—that I'm not as good as you are?

Sometimes administration can inadvertently pit one teacher against another—we need a common goal and purpose.

[It may inspire] jealousy, mainly due to the other's success. It'll be difficult for me to hear that the other person succeeded while I didn't always succeed.

Teachers explained that staff members aspire to learn and advance, but competition may hinder such learning. When teachers' performance in schools is measured in relation to successes, some will be reluctant to share their secrets to success with perceived competitors:

Sometimes people don't want to share—they're more concerned about being a shining star.

—an elementary school music teacher

There are people who don't like to share success, not wanting their colleagues to do what they do. These are people who work alone and don't go in for teamwork, because that way they can continue to stand out and be better than others.

—a middle school biology teacher

I feel that not everyone is always open to the subject [of successes] and to this nature of learning. Not everyone likes to share their success with others or to give others credit and partake in their success.

—a high school English teacher

There is the issue of the desire to maintain a monopoly.

—an elementary school homeroom teacher

> Professional knowledge is often kept as discreet as atom bomb secrets.
>
> —a high school physics teacher

Apprehensiveness about the possibility of exposure and ensuing criticism was mentioned extensively by teachers at all school levels. Teachers asserted that a competitive atmosphere between staff members may cause strain between colleagues or that negative relationships might diminish the possibilities for the healthy kind of competition in which individuals all strive for success and one's accomplishments are viewed as the success of the whole organization and vice versa:

> The successful teachers are apprehensive about analyzing their success in front of their colleagues. . . . It might cause tension.
>
> —a middle school science teacher

> By nature, I'm open to hearing about others' success, and I like to learn from others' ideas. I know there are people around me who find it hard to cope with others' success and to utilize what may be learned from it. That's how people become hesitant about sharing experiences of success. Instead of understanding that it will contribute to the staff, they're afraid to talk because it might sound too much like they're patting themselves on the back.
>
> —a middle school art teacher

In contrast, teachers related competitiveness as being potentially stimulating, motivating, and positive as well. Various teachers noted how a competitive atmosphere creates opportunities for mutually enriching learning, enabling the creation of a model for comparison and drawing conclusions:

> On the other hand, it [learning from success] could have the opposite effect, of imparting tools, giving the team new ideas. That is, I want to create success in a particular situation or with a particular student. So as soon as I hear this one [teacher] say something and that one [teacher] say something, I can adopt those successful ideas and practices. I can adopt them for my own use and maybe they will work for me. It's good to hear that other teachers are successful.
>
> —an elementary school homeroom teacher

> Seeing the positive and being able to project it into other areas is necessary. In the short run, what is needed is mutual encouragement on the one hand and possibly also positive competition.
>
> —an elementary school grade-level coordinator

> If I hear from a teacher that a specific act of his was successful, I imitate him. If teachers sit and talk about another teacher who has achieved some sort of success, I learn from it and follow in her footsteps.
>
> —an elementary school English coordinator

TALK ABOUT EXPERIENCE

Another issue that interviewees highlighted was the relationship between new and veteran teachers. Teachers reported that differences in experience can impede learning from success because new teachers may feel threatened by veterans, and the latter may disparage inexperienced teachers:

> Talking about learning from success could cause stress for certain people in the system as well as strife for the senior teachers, who are burnt out and not interested in investing effort in their work, contrary to the new teachers who come to work full of pep. . . . Some senior teachers, old-timers who are set in their ways, don't see success as something to be proud of or investigated. Such teachers might block others' success, causing discouragement and an unpleasant atmosphere for the whole teacher body, and sometimes this will influence teachers to refrain from talking about their success or to make little of successes, if they mention them at all.
>
> —an elementary school math teacher

> I don't think staff members are willing to embark on and experience this sort of process of joint learning from success. There's a nucleus of senior teachers who are very experienced, they've learned from their experience and they rely on their expertise and knowledge. It's hard to change the structure of the system after so many years; I don't know if it'll happen. Maybe we should try a senior teacher coaching a new teacher so that both can learn from each other's successes.
>
> —a middle school pedagogical coordinator

In sum, regarding schools' culture of learning, a negative atmosphere and relationships—including tensions, envy, or competitiveness—were reported as key factors inhibiting learning from success. On the other hand, interviewees asserted that teachers' active participation in learning from success is linked with positive faculty relationships (e.g., openness, trust, and support) and a positive, mutually respectful climate within which to share one's successes with other teachers despite the perceived risk of exposure involved in this process. Teachers spoke of the need to develop a learning group in an atmosphere of kindness and acceptance. They stressed the need to overcome a lack of openness, empathy, and willingness to share. These recommendations by teachers recognize humans' defensive routines during organizational social endeavors, which inhibit members from expressing and testing their assumptions (Argyris & Schon, 1996; Louis, 2006). This calls for an atmosphere of generosity and acceptance, especially with regard to defining what counts as success in the collective learning arena.

Importantly, teachers sometimes expressed their concern that learning from success might pose a threat to their professional status in the eyes of the other faculty members, including apprehension about occupational repercussions from their superiors. They described an anti-learning culture prevailing in their schools, which manifests itself in fear of criticism and worry about placing one's professional legitimacy at stake. It is possible that teachers' analysis of successes in public may tend to stimulate reflection of a comparative nature between one's own professional knowledge and skills and those of colleagues. When teachers compare the competencies presented in their peers' successful practices with their own professional work and skills, they may come to perceive themselves as less capable professionally, thus reducing perceived self-efficacy or vice versa. By extension, as perceived self- and collective-efficacy influence one another in reciprocal ways (Goddard, Goddard, Kim, & Miller, 2015), collective learning from success can revitalize or demoralize faculty's shared belief in its conjoint capabilities to organize and execute the courses of action needed to attain their school's mission.

2. DEFINING THE TERM SUCCESS

Different people define *success* according to different criteria. What one teacher considers to be a success may not be considered successful by another or may even be regarded as failure. One of the factors hindering the process of collective learning from success, according to teachers (mentioned by 56.5% of the interviewed teachers), was the issue of how the term *success* should actually be defined:

> Sometimes what I think of as success is not what someone else sees as such. So, if people are not on the same wavelength, it's really hard. Although we have
>
> *(Continued)*

(Continued)

cooperation here, and each of us enriches the other and I see it as a positive thing, it's also problematic because what one teacher sees as success is not seen that way by others.

—a middle school social science coordinator

Different definitions of the concept of success can cause tensions and competition among teachers:

If the other teachers feel that my success is not what they see as success, they might make fun of me.

—a high school grade-level coordinator

A teacher exposes others to actions or events that he thought were successful, and their outcomes proved it to be true. On the other hand, he may be alerted to additional opinions, to points he didn't think of, or to criticism.

—an elementary school homeroom teacher

I have no problem sharing, but I do have a problem with those who say, "Why is she getting all excited about her own success?" Or they say, "Is that a success? Not for me. For me, that's just normal, and if she doesn't do that all the time, she's not a good teacher." That's my dilemma.

—a middle school homeroom teacher

Sometimes a person can see something as a success while another sees it as obvious, and then the first one will be hesitant about publicizing or sharing it.

—an elementary school homeroom teacher

Sometimes staff members can perceive success from different points of view, which could lead to arguments and conflicts among them.

—a middle school Bible teacher

> I can certainly imagine how this process can cause some staff members to sense tension and fear . . . and also the possibility of creating negative competition, with everyone wanting to present their successful actions—in their eyes—which are not always regarded as such by their colleagues. It's also inhibiting when others don't believe your story or do not accept it as a success story. Then you get insulted and no longer want to share. Not every teacher has the same character, not every work method suits me or you, and someone else's way to success is not necessarily appropriate for me.
>
> —a high school homeroom teacher and social activity coordinator

A number of teachers noted that a method leading to success by one teacher does not always work for others:

> If we talk about success, that same so-called success can be a failure for another teacher, which is frustrating.
>
> —a middle school English teacher

> Success is a personal matter. I can succeed with a certain child, and another person will not succeed with him or her. There are situations in the classroom where there is one teacher who will succeed and another who won't, so a certain method can suit her but not me . . . this can create a kind of competition.
>
> —an elementary school homeroom teacher

Overall, various teachers noted that the absence of a clear, objective definition of the term *success* may cause tensions and competition among teachers. Interviewees argued that usually the school staff differs on values and beliefs regarding successful professional activities. Thus, an action perceived as successful by one team member may be considered less successful or even a failure by another teacher. Inability to agree on the definition of *success* may prevent teachers from sharing successes, and thus teachers may miss opportunities to learn from success.

3. Focus on Tests and Assessments

One major factor hindering learning from success was identified as schools' heavy emphasis on assessing students through in-school and standard examinations, in line with externally imposed educational assessment programs (as mentioned by 51.5% of the interviewed teachers). The learning culture of schools is inherently influenced by the demands posed by supervisors and policymakers at the district and national levels, who define schools' success in terms of a relatively narrow prism of student achievements. Interviewed teachers consistently reported that they experienced pressures and constraints on their work stemming from their schools' heavy focus on tests and assessments, which limited their opportunities to learn from successes. Teachers felt they were not encouraged to share successes with peers other than those strictly related to the desired improvements in standard academic achievements:

> I don't think we do that [learning from success] enough in the school. It is more focused on tests and building standard assessments and not on what successes have occurred in classrooms, what has worked in classrooms. . . . When you are not working on building standard assessments, you have more time to focus on other things.
>
> —a high school grade-level coordinator

Interviewees asserted that the system's contemporary focus on assessment standards and accountability relieves teachers of full responsibility over their teaching. Instead, the standards for success remain in the hands of higher authorities, who set top-down expectations for teacher behavior. This state of affairs was seen by our interviewees as interfering with teachers' own efforts to learn from successes and to implement the bottom-up insights thereby gained.

> I think we have to shift our thinking away from standardization. . . . I think learning from our successes would get us away from the notion of standardization and put the ownership and responsibility on the shoulders of the teachers.
>
> —a middle school history teacher

One outcome of learning environments that focuses on tests and assessments is that short-term successes are examined. One high school physics teacher claimed that learning from success is a long-term process, while under the current policy, teachers are being measured based on immediate successes:

> It takes time to shift culture like this, and sometimes school reform efforts need to show immediate successful results in order for high-up administration and the board of education to keep the reform going.

THE COLLECTIVE WISDOM OF PRACTICE

In sum, teachers mentioned their schools' focus on assessments as limiting flexibility in their teaching and as hindering learning from success. They described the current era of imposed standards and accountability as a major factor inhibiting an inquiry-based learning culture (Giles & Hargreaves, 2006). These perceptions are important, as schools do not operate in a vacuum; they function as part of a larger social system, including the school district and the local community in which they are embedded. In addition, teachers felt that the emphasis on testing left little space in the school culture for creating and maintaining organizational mechanisms that would offer them possibilities for learning collectively and changing their ways of teaching (for more on this, see "5. Organizational Resources" below).

4. Leadership for Learning

The role of the school's administration as a force acting from above constituted a significant factor for interviewed teachers (mentioned by 43.5% of the interviewees), alternatively motivating or inhibiting teachers' collective learning from success. The school principal and administrative staff have the ability to motivate and speed up the process of learning from success if they devote the proper work, trust in the process, and recruit staff members effectively to participate. On the other hand, learning from success may be inhibited by a school administration's lack of motivation, inappropriate intervention, or arbitrary imposition of this habit of practice onto the staff. The learning-from-success process begins at the top of the school hierarchy, from the administration, and goes all the way down to the teaching staff. If school principals believe in the process and sweep their teachers along with them, it will work. Interviewed teachers emphasized the importance of the principal's role and pinpointed the principal's personality as a significant factor:

> The most important element is the principal who's at the top of the pyramid. If the principal believes in this process, it'll work. . . . Once the principal demonstrates his or her faith in and acceptance of the process, teachers will feel safer devoting themselves to it.
>
> —an elementary school pedagogical coordinator

> If the process is to materialize, the school's administration must push it. Only this will get the teachers to express their willingness to participate, otherwise it has no chance. The principal's personality is also important. In my opinion, a principal has to believe in the abilities of his staff, allowing processes to unfold even when his control of both the process and its products is not total. It should
>
> *(Continued)*

(Continued)

be a principal with lots of self-confidence, who has a good relationship with the staff while also enjoying the trust and approval of his superiors.

—a high school biology teacher

The school principal's attitude and behavior in this context—Does she encourage learning from success? Does she talk about it?—I think it all begins from here, from how the principal presents it. Of course, it has to be in cooperation with the educational staff, otherwise it might just fade away.

—a high school math teacher

As voiced by interviewed teachers, the school administration's motivation and leadership style is tightly connected to the staff's cooperation:

First of all, the principal is the one who can make it happen. She can't do it alone. She needs the staff to lead it along with her, to think how it'll function on the ground, what it'll look like, to build some clear plan, maybe hold some sort of meeting or two to instill the value of it all in us, and then to go ahead with it. Of course, it also requires a lot of teamwork and cooperation.

—a high school homeroom teacher

I believe that a decision made from above by a strong principal, with the backing of the superintendent, . . . can indeed greatly advance its realization. At the same time, the principal must give every member of the team the opportunity to succeed and thereby drive a process of learning from success in the school. Then, as a result, a discussion will ensue about these successes and their causes.

—a high school math coordinator

Although the school principal constitutes a crucial factor in facilitating the process of learning from success, the administration may also hinder the process through improper and unhealthy interference in teacher relationships:

If the administration intervenes in teachers' discourse, it will disturb them. The mere appearance of the principal can cause some teachers to boast and glorify themselves. . . . It all depends on the principal's attitude at the first meeting. It all depends on how she responds to learning from teachers' success. Her attitude is the factor that will motivate teachers to open up, share, and inquire into their success or to shut down and keep quiet.

—a high school science teacher

If a principal takes teachers' personal stories, situations, and practices and goes on to use them in a negative way, he or she may discourage the process of learning from success.

—an elementary school homeroom teacher

Teachers noted that the principal's overt intervention in how the collective learning process unfolds via "instructions from above" might thwart or delay learning from success:

It's important to get the project going right from the beginning of the year, and not to just impose it from above but rather to explain its rationale in detail and to outline how the process should be conducted, emphasizing its positive points. When it's happening right from the beginning of the year, it's important that it should come from teachers so that they see their need for it. . . . It's important to think about how to present it, not as an isolated meeting once in a while but rather as part and parcel of a culture or climate; teachers should feel they're gaining from it and that there is someone from the administration who will check on it. . . . It must be gradually woven into the school fabric, so to speak, so that teachers don't feel that this is just another burden or pressure.

—a middle school social science coordinator

The school administration's role as a driving force from above is reflected in the utterances of teachers who distinguished voluntary participation from forced participation in the learning-from-success process. Various teachers noted that voluntary participation, namely teachers' free choice to participate in the process, is a factor that can speed up and promote realization of the collective learning from success in the school:

Teachers won't mind cooperating because they are participating willingly and are not forced to . . . when it comes from their own free will and not by orders

(Continued)

(Continued)

of the administration. How can cooperation be expected when one is being forced, even if we deal with our successes? The course has to be open to those who want it.

—a high school chemistry teacher

It seems to me now that the fact that we will be forced to attend a meeting aimed at learning from success might lead to some teachers just closing up instead of opening up and sharing. Learning from success must be done voluntarily, with people you feel comfortable and secure with, because otherwise true and sincere learning from each other just won't happen.

—an elementary school history teacher

The teachers should be partners in this process that is about to take place. The moment something is forced from above [means] there's not enough cooperation or deep involvement.

—a middle school grade-level coordinator

First of all, teachers should agree to participate in such a process; it should be voluntary, not something that's forced or mandatory. . . . I think it should come from the teachers' own will.

—a high school homeroom teacher

In sum, the school administrators play a decisive and significant role in facilitating or impeding schools' process of collective learning from success. Teachers opined that the school administration has the ability to motivate and accelerate or alternatively thwart or delay collective learning processes at school. The administration's faith in the process, readiness for teamwork, and ability to motivate staff are significant in this context. It was also argued that the principal's perception of the process of learning from success and his or her ability to attract the school staff and thus create a school discourse revolving around learning from success are crucial.

5. Organizational Resources: Time and Focus/Prioritization

In order to achieve optimal collective learning from success, interviewed teachers claimed that two major organizational resources are crucial: sufficient and appropriate time allocations and changes in the school's priority setting. Organizational resources were mentioned by 39.5% of the interviewed teachers as a major determinant of learning from success.

TIME RESOURCES

Interviewed teachers agreed that time is a crucial factor in driving the process of learning from success. In order for the learning-from-success process to be structured and professional, it must be granted proper amounts of time, fixed scheduling considerations, and appropriate conditions that take teachers' busy work schedule into account:

> Let's start with the technical part. Meetings in which learning from success is practiced should be set at a certain hour, I mean, at a fixed time.
>
> —a high school math/computers coordinator

> Conditions, time, time, time . . . a specific time is a very important factor here.
>
> —an elementary school art teacher

> They shouldn't bring me to meetings like this in the evening. They should be scheduled as part of our work hours and defined as such.
>
> —an elementary school special education teacher

> I think we need to have a clear schedule; it has to be organized. . . . They should designate time in the schedule to hold these meetings, so that these conversations will not be held during recess, or at the end of the day, because then we can't stay at school. Let's be realistic. We need it to be built into the system, maybe an hour a week. Then the teachers will take it seriously.
>
> —a high school homeroom teacher

> I think it takes time. As you know, teachers find it very difficult to make time. They are so busy. This system is overloaded. There are lots of meetings; it's a great burden. So, you prioritize. . . . I think if we have time and motivation, there's no reason why it shouldn't work.
>
> —an elementary school science teacher

Teachers noted that a set, predefined time for collective learning from success is a vital precondition in order for the process to materialize. Similarly, interviewees argued that when such a time is not available, and when basic conditions are not met to allow ample time for learning from successes, it is difficult for teachers and staff to attain meaningful learning:

> Three years ago, I would open each teachers' meeting with a round of teachers recounting their success stories. Today, we look at the clock more than we look at content.
>
> —a high school math coordinator

> At teachers' meetings, which are the natural time for discourse on learning from success, more immediate and urgent needs come up, so that we don't have time to discuss success but instead we are busy "putting out fires."
>
> —a high school English teacher

Thus, educators stressed that the way the school day is organized limits the possibility of creating formal collective learning processes. Interviewees pointed out that in order to succeed in a collective learning-from-success process, they need structured time during their working hours.

PRIORITIZATION OF LEARNING FROM SUCCESS

Various schools and their faculties uphold different priorities for the given time-frame at their disposal, which may influence how learning from success is implemented in a particular school. Depending on where learning from success is positioned among schools' main foci, the schools' prioritization may delay or alternatively speed up the process of learning from success. Interviewees called for high prioritization of learning from success, as shown in the following excerpts:

> In my opinion, the process can be successful and beneficial. However, we must examine its place in the range of school activities and courses. That is, it should be given a place of honor and not added on as an afterthought, constituting a burden on the staff. What can hinder this project of learning from success is work overload. Multiple programs, multiple challenges. . . . It is of first and foremost importance that we define the subject as part of the school's goals at the administration team level. The next stage will be an attempt to integrate

this activity into the school agenda and give it priority. Of course, we need proper guidance to lead the process.

—a middle school grade-level coordinator

I think we should consider this in a focused way. That means that if the school decides to go for learning from success, it may be necessary to give up other projects. Not too long ago, we entered a national reform program. It takes a lot of effort. But it seems to me that what is special about learning from success is this subject's relevance to every other field of activity in the school. In fact, it is not an independent topic but rather a framework accompanying all other fields.

—an elementary school science teacher

Other interviewees pointed out why prioritization might impede the implementation of collective learning practices:

You have to be crazy about this project. . . . People have to have the time for it. . . . There are too many new things that have entered schools, and this makes for some burnout.

—a middle school science coordinator

There are always important and urgent things coming up like national exams, visits to the school which mean a great deal of work for the staff, new programs imposed on us by the Ministry of Education, and we have to meet their objectives. . . . All this makes it even more difficult to talk about learning from our successes.

—a high school math teacher

In sum, teachers argued that adequate organizational resources are a vital condition for learning. Specifically, time is a crucial factor to permit collective learning in general and to enable learning from success in particular. Noting their enormous workload of pressing issues, teachers claimed that in order to maintain learning from success, appropriate time should be devoted to it and it should be highly prioritized and integrated into the school agenda. Collective learning at school requires allocation of adequate, dedicated time for teachers' meetings, with fixed times and places for it to happen. If, in fact, no specific place and time are allocated and maintained for learning from success, then the decision to engage in such learning will merely remain wishful thinking (Sykes, Rosenfeld, & Weiss, 2006).

MINDSCAPES OF ADDITIONAL
ECHELONS IN THE EDUCATION SYSTEM

To furnish a wider perspective, it is important to illuminate how different stakeholders in the educational system—other than in-service teachers—perceive collective learning from success. Several research studies are briefly reported next, examining the views expressed by superintendents, in-service principals, prospective principals, teacher mentors, and prospective teachers concerning the collective learning-from-success process.

A qualitative study analyzing the perceptions of 61 district superintendents (Schechter, 2011a) underscored their concern that attempts to implement learning from success would flounder due to the predominant lack of a learning culture in the educational system, a culture in which educators could be generous in sharing their capabilities. Superintendents even described a contemporary anti-learning culture in their schools, which manifests itself in stakeholders' fears about the learning-from-success process—fear of criticism, fear of having one's professional legitimacy threatened, and so on. Moreover, superintendents claimed that it is impossible to carve time for collective learning from success when working with principals and faculty members because superintendents must focus their limited time and attention squarely on solving urgent problems. Thus, in light of their time constraints, urgent priorities, and work overload, superintendents do not have the opportunity to deliberate with principals and teachers on their own successes, especially in the current era of accountability. In other words, eradicating problems in an atmosphere of accountability must take highest priority, thereby limiting the allocation of time and resources to be dedicated to active involvement in formal, long-term learning-from-success processes.

Another qualitative study (Schechter, 2011c) examined the perceptions of 65 in-service principals, spanning a wide range of experience levels in elementary, middle, and high schools, concerning the notion and strategy of collective learning from practitioners' successful practices. These principals argued that in contrast to collective learning processes that aim to evaluate failures and problems, collective learning from successful practices requires a deliberate and conscious shift in mindset with regard to collaborative learning in schools. Principals perceived the competitive culture and the continual comparisons of professional abilities among faculty members as potentially major obstacles to a productive process of collective learning from success. Moreover, these principals perceived the changing external demands imposed by district officials, especially by school superintendents, as a major obstacle to a productive process of collective learning from success.

In another qualitative study (Schechter, 2008b), prospective principals voiced concern about implementing collective learning from success as a leadership strategy due to the process's possible effects on teachers' sense of self-efficacy. On the other hand, according to these university students enrolled in a principal preparatory program, an intentional focus on past successes could indeed have beneficial outcomes: It could bring to light positive recognition of teachers' expertise that underlies their successes, thereby fostering a belief in their capacity to succeed in their tasks and to learn from their experiences. However, prospective principals in this leadership program estimated that the same learning process could lead to a downward, negative pattern if teachers perceived themselves as less professionally capable compared to the competencies presented in their peers' successful practices.

Similarly, both teacher mentors and prospective teachers (Schechter & Michael, 2014) expressed unease about applying the collective learning-from-success process in their future schools due to its likely negative impact on prospective teachers' sense of self-efficacy. Both mentors and student teachers estimated that the learning process of inquiring into successful practices in the collective arena (with a mentor or with a mentor and peers [other student teachers]) could lead to a negative pattern if prospective teachers perceived themselves as less professionally capable compared to their peers who might present, in describing their successful practices, competencies that the prospective teachers do not yet possess.

In sum, this chapter explored educators' various mindscapes regarding the collective learning-from-success process, providing implications for its potential implementation and maintenance. Thus, through teachers' perceptions as well as the perceptions of other echelons in the education system (superintendents, in-service principals, prospective principals, teacher mentors, and prospective teachers), this chapter illuminated the conditions necessary for igniting collective learning processes in school systems. These mindscapes clearly call for a well-designed collective journey that focuses on continuous processes of learning from educators' professional successes.

CHAPTER 4

The Learning-From-Success Journey

Enacting Wisdom

> By three methods we may learn wisdom: First, by reflection, which is noblest; second, by imitation, which is easiest; and third, by experience, which is the bitterest.
>
> —Confucius

> We started talking about success. Previously, we had focused on problems, failures, and difficulties. We discovered that we also know how to succeed and especially how to learn from it. This was our turning point.
>
> —an elementary math teacher

> The learning-from-success program is structured and clear. Participants get in touch with their insights about their successes, study, and analyze them. This is a useful tool for developing a different organizational culture.
>
> —a high school principal

Jona Rosenfeld has worked and written for many years on issues related to learning from success and its importance for the development of successful interventions that can target those populations lying on the margins of society

(Rosenfeld, 1996, 1997; Rosenfeld & Krim, 1983; Rosenfeld, Schon, & Sykes, 1995; Rosenfeld & Tardieu, 2000). The rationale for Rosenfeld's learning-from-success orientation was his recognition of many instances in which people who were living in deep poverty and hopelessness had nevertheless been helped to reconnect with society and to lead productive lives. Even if such incidents represented a relatively rare occurrence, Rosenfeld identified them as an oft-missed learning opportunity because too few of the relevant people involved with such marginal populations had noticed and analyzed these rare but impressive successes.

Rosenfeld and his colleagues asserted that the true key to learning from success required a shift from the complacency of *selective inattention*—whereby successful practices are often ignored by professionals and researchers—to the deliberate focus of *selective attention* onto these very practices in order to uncover the implicit wisdom of practice that made them happen. Importantly, Rosenfeld, Sykes, and their group then clarified the optimal means for uncovering the implicit structure underlying the practice of learning from success. On the basis of this framework, they formulated the learning-from-success journey (Ellenbogen-Frankovits, Shemer, & Rosenfeld, 2011; Rosenfeld, Sykes, Weiss, & Dolev, 2002; Sykes, Rosenfeld, & Weiss, 2006) that can allow educational systems to enact their own wisdoms of best practices.

This chapter leads readers into the *learning-from-success journey*—a structured multicomponent framework for collaborative inquiry into professional successes that may provide the impetus for significant change in schools. The learning-from-success journey, as it has developed over the years, contains a number of different but complementary components: (a) the format for inquiry into successes, (b) the strategies for learning from success, (c) identifying who the learning-from-success group should be, (d) the documentation needed for dissemination of products and outcomes, and (e) the evaluation of the process as a whole. This chapter elaborates on each of these components.

A. THE MULTISTEP FORMAT FOR INQUIRY: THE COLLABORATIVE JOURNEY

How can schools design a journey of learning from success? How can researchers and policymakers motivate educators to undertake such a journey in order to enhance their capacity to learn from their own professional successes? The essence of the learning-from-success journey is a school's introduction of a structured process of reflection concerning its previous successful actions. This is something that educators very often do not take the time to initiate or perform. Moreover, the effect of such a journey is highly amplified by the fact that it occurs in a peer group setting. The power of the group is manifested in everyone contributing and receiving. The group helps each of its members to better understand and learn from their own experience and to discover additional perspectives and points of view. Thus, not only does each group member learn for himself or herself but each person also teaches or inspires the others. Within this duality, each member of the collective becomes at once both a learner and a sharer of experiences, a benefactor and a beneficiary of knowledge, one who enhances and at the same time benefits from the collaborative inquiry.

At the heart of the collaborative inquiry lies the following challenge: How is it possible to guide groups in their learning about a complex activity—one that has multiple goals, contexts, and partners over a long duration—in a way that is fruitful and sustained? To meet this challenge, the learning-from-success journey constitutes a structured process with a characteristic inquiry format (Schechter, Sykes, & Rosenfeld, 2008; Sykes et al., 2006). This multistep format is designed to guide the group's learning process by systematically making participants aware of selected aspects of inquiry at defined stages of the journey.

The inquiry format should be viewed as a sort of map that can facilitate a group's ability to learn from complex past endeavors and occurrences so that the group members can extract knowledge from them. This knowledge may contribute to the production of future successful actions in other contexts. A complex endeavor or occurrence refers to activities that have manifold aims, contexts, and stakeholders while unfolding over an extended period of time. Although a collective learning group may possibly perform part of its inquiry into a complex subject during a single session, a complete collaborative learning process generally requires several sessions. Furthermore, to maximize the effectiveness of the learning process, collective learning from success should also include preparation before each session, group reflection, and additional learning produced by documenting the products of the group reflection.

Specifically, the learning-from-success format for inquiry consists of nine steps. Each step represents a strategy for overcoming potential obstacles in the process of collective learning from the group members' successes. Most importantly, these steps are distinct but highly related in a spiral motion ascending toward eliciting the group's wisdom of practice. As illustrated in Figure 4.1, these nine steps are listed in progressive order starting from the bottom and rising to the top, but they should be perceived as a cyclical, dynamic, and interactive process of inquiry.

STEP 1. IDENTIFY AREAS OF SUCCESS
WITHIN THE ORGANIZATIONAL CONTEXT

The first step in learning from success is to identify an individual, group, or organizational enterprise that can be considered a success of sufficient significance to be a worthy subject for in-depth examination and learning processes. In some organizational contexts, this initial step, simple as it may seem, constitutes a barrier.

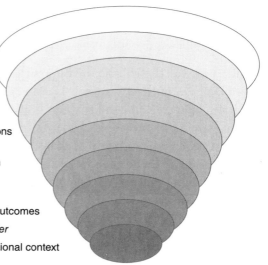

9. Experiment and disseminate

8. Identify issues for further study

7. Craft key principles of action based on the
   successful actions

6. Choose critical turning points and detail the actions
   to success

5. Identify turning points or milestones on the path
   to success

4. Describe negative consequences

3. Describe the positive objective and subjective outcomes

2. Describe the success in terms of *before* and *after*

1. Identify the area of success within the organizational context

Many cultures (organizational or otherwise) do not encourage the recognition of success for a variety of reasons, such as attribution of high value to modesty, fear of arousing envy, fear of appearing to brag, a tendency to focus on failures or mistakes, or mere habit (Gino & Pisano, 2011; Rosenfeld et al., 2002; Schechter, 2012). That said, in any organization, learning from success may arouse anxieties concerning the question of whether successes actually exist within the organization. Therefore, this first step of seeking out instances to label as successes is often important in and of itself because it begins the shift of attention toward successes in the organization.

Which Successes Should Be Chosen for Group Inquiry?

The initial search for successes in schools requires guidance, particularly when attempting to select successes that can appropriately serve a long-term collective learning process. In investigating possible candidate events or experiences, it is preferable to begin with small successes at the individual, dyadic, or group level rather than starting out with more complex systemwide successes. The following are some important characteristics of a successful experience, enterprise, or event that may be deemed worthy of study in school organizations (Sykes et al., 2006):

- The achievement of positive outcomes can be traced to deliberate professional actions.

- The success promoted achievement of the organization's mission as well as contributed, directly or indirectly, to students.

- The success was accomplished under significantly difficult conditions.

- There is objective evidence (preferably measurable) of success.

- There is subjective evidence (e.g., satisfaction of those involved) of success.

How Should Inquiry Groups Identify Successes?

What is the basic process through which the school learning group's facilitator proceeds to identify a success worthy of group learning? Two such basic processes have been identified. One relies on the members of the learning group: The facilitator may ask group participants to briefly describe successes with which they are familiar from their own work, and then the facilitator can decide together with them which to investigate jointly.

Alternatively, a second process for identifying successes for study relies on the facilitator's prior acquaintance with organizational members and their work. Prior to the learning group's first meeting, the facilitator may cull successes from personal conversations with school staff members, determine which success will best serve the group's learning process, and prepare one or more successes ahead of time for the group to investigate. In this case, to determine the advisability of selecting a candidate success for group learning, the facilitator will hold a preliminary inquiry in line with the multistep inquiry format, including an initial clarification of outcomes and costs as well as consideration of who else played an important part in the success and should therefore be present at the group session (Ellenbogen-Frankovits et al., 2011).

STEP 2. LOOK AT CHANGE: DESCRIBE THE SUCCESS IN TERMS OF A COMPARISON BETWEEN *BEFORE* AND *AFTER*

For the second step in the multistep inquiry format, once a success has been identified and selected for collective learning in the previous step, participants are asked to provide a concise description of the situation at hand *before* and *after* the endeavor was undertaken. Explicit examination of the *before* and *after* highlights for the group—those changes that have taken place over time, namely a view of the success in a broad timeframe—underscores developments through a temporal sequence. Thus, this step of inquiry enables group members to acquire a bird's eye view that takes in the whole picture from start to finish (Sykes et al., 2006). In this comparison of a particular school situation *before* versus the same situation *after*, any discovery of significant positive changes over time would indicate the probability that successful actions have indeed taken place. For example, the following were descriptors given by group members to depict the *before* situation in the case of a junior high school's success in reducing school violence:

- There were many reports by teachers and students about violence—harassment, assaults, curses, threats.

- The focal points of violence were in the restrooms, on the way home from school, in the schoolyard, and in the classroom during recess.

- The school had the reputation of being a violent place.

In contrast, the following descriptors were given to depict the case in the same junior high school *after* the successful violence-reducing actions were taken:

- There has been a sharp decline in formal reports of violent incidents.

- The teachers complain less about violent incidents.

- The parents and those coming to the school say that the scholastic atmosphere is very good and that they have not encountered violence.

- There is an open and ongoing dialogue in the school about violence.

In sum, this *before* versus *after* comparison step assures the group's establishment of the underlying framework for inquiry. This initial framework is established through the following three directives:

1. Provide a concise description of the process that is being referred to as a success.

2. Set aside, at this stage, the processes through which success was achieved.

3. Highlight the changes that took place as a result of the success.

STEP 3. FOCUS ON THE POSITIVE: DESCRIBE POSITIVE OBJECTIVE AND SUBJECTIVE OUTCOMES

In this third step of the inquiry process, the group reflects more deeply and critically upon how it determines success in an attempt to pinpoint the particular outcomes that were achieved in the success story being analyzed. Expanding and deepening the investigation of outcomes enables the group to construct a clear picture of the nature of those changes that can be attributed to a studied success. The strategy here is to flesh out previously unrecognized objective indicators of success that are measurable (when possible) as well as subjective indicators of success.

Such indicators can be uncovered by deliberately scanning personal, interpersonal, functional, procedural, and systemic realms of experience. Thus, positive outcomes can be objective or subjective, and they may or may not be measurable. They may also transpire at several levels: (a) within individuals—in their behaviors, feelings, or cognitions; (b) between individuals—in their quality of relationships, communication, or team performance; or (c) at the organizational process level (Rosenfeld et al., 2002).

An example of positive outcomes gleaned via collective learning from one high school's success in dealing with students' poor mathematics achievements may serve as an illustration. One high school encountered a situation in which a substantial subset of all three of its grade levels (Grades 10–12)—about 20 to 30 students per grade—was failing math. These students' average math grades below 40 (out of 100) raised the school's concern as to these students' ability to pass the upcoming math matriculation exam. At this third step of the collective inquiry format, without focusing on the successful practices themselves yet, the learning group identified both objective and subjective outcomes of the studied success. The school's two *objective positive outcomes* comprised its improvement in students' achievements as measured by higher percentages of students who fulfilled the requirements for a matriculation certificate and an increase in students' attendance. The three *subjective positive outcomes* comprised an improved climate in class, more positive student attitudes toward the math subjects being learned, and greater trust of the community in the school faculty and administration.

STEP 4. DESCRIBE NEGATIVE CONSEQUENCES

The decision that a particular professional action was successful cannot be based solely on evidence of positive changes. It must also be grounded in an unflinching recognition of coexisting negative consequences and of the extent to which the organization had to invest precious resources in order to achieve those positive outcomes—the cost–benefit ratio. The existence of negative consequences does not contradict the possibility that the actions at hand were indeed successful. The extent to which a set of actions can be defined as a success is determined by weighing positive outcomes against the obvious as well as the more hidden consequences (Rosenfeld et al., 2002; Sykes et al., 2006).

At the fourth step in the multistep inquiry format, the learning group is asked to consider the resources invested by the school to obtain this success and the negative consequences of achieving the change that was described in the earlier steps. Thus, the quality and value of past success as a basis for learning can only be determined by rigorously assessing positive and negative outcomes. Negative outcomes may include harm to individuals who have lost out or been left behind, backlash that threatens the viability of the change or of its advocates, and the burden of study hours on weak students who experience attention difficulties.

With regard to the previous illustration on the high school that encountered a substantial subset of failing math students across all grade levels, the collective learning group identified negative outcomes associated with what had been initially defined as a successful practice. Two negative outcomes were noted: decline in students' achievements in other subject matters, such as history and geography, and students' low motivation to invest effort in non-matriculation activities, such as community service. Delineating the negative outcomes enabled the learning group to now rigorously weigh the benefits versus the costs of the school enterprise being analyzed.

STEP 5. IDENTIFY TURNING POINTS OR MILESTONES ON THE PATH TO SUCCESS

In this step of the inquiry format, the group directs its attention away from the *before* (problem) and the *after* (positive and negative outcomes) and begins to dissect the actual core of the success: the *process* through which positive outcomes were achieved. Success stories often encompass a complex series of actions taken over extended periods of time. The facilitator needs to help the group break them down into manageable, chronologically ordered stages, marked off by crucial turning points and key milestones.

This step establishes an intermediate framework for viewing the success along its chronological timeline. Step 6 delves further into the specific actions occurring at each of these key points of time, but here, the focus is on initially recognizing which times along the successful long-term process appear to be meaningful milestones that will be particularly fruitful for continued focused inquiry. Turning points or milestones are best identified by introducing the following assertions to the learning group:

- Very few successes in complex areas of human services, especially in education, take place linearly, with one step leading directly to the next all the way to the end.

- Instead, success is frequently the outcome of successfully managing nonlinear processes of change, where you as practitioners must often discover your own venues for action.

- Such key turning points for action emerge during your own interactions within your specific contexts.

- Viewed retrospectively, such milestones along the nonlinear path to change can help deepen understanding of the complexities underlying successful practices.

These turning points or milestones might include, for instance, the school's introduction of inputs from external sources (such as significant successful changes in personnel) or they might refer to certain professional actions that helped overcome conditions seen as an impasse that had blocked progress in a desired direction (Ellenbogen-Frankovits et al., 2011; Sykes et al., 2006). For example, the aforementioned learning group that discussed the junior high school facing acts of student violence such as theft, hooliganism, vandalism, bullying, and physical aggression identified the following turning points in the school's success at lowering levels of violence:

- Recruiting relevant parties—teachers, parents (e.g., parents' committee), and students (e.g., student council)—and establishing dialogue with these parties to generate constructive suggestions and formulate a violence-reducing school policy with broad support

- Identifying the most aggressive subgroup of students

- Conducting one-on-one work by teachers with these identified aggressive students

- Fostering this subgroup's transition from violent students to responsible students by (a) assigning them specific duties at official school events and (b) appointing them as escorts for children on their way home from school

- Establishing a joint soccer team between two rival cliques that had been fighting in the school

As can be seen from this case illustration, outlining a list of such turning points or milestones that occurred during the successful school enterprise is an important step for the inquiry process. Next, the group needs to locate which specific actions occurred at those turning points considered to be critical in nature.

STEP 6. CHOOSE TURNING POINTS THAT WERE CRITICAL AND DETAIL THE ACTIONS THAT LED TO SUCCESS

This step can be considered the heart of the learning journey. All previous steps set the stage for this one, in which participants in the success are guided by the group facilitator to reconstruct the details of events and actions that were critical to its achievement. It is within this very detail that the wisdom of practice can be uncovered. These are the specific actions and action strategies that are generally difficult for practitioners to retrieve on their own but are nonetheless crucially reflected in practitioners' successful outcomes (Sykes et al., 2006).

The focal point at this step of inquiry is *action talk*—discourse focusing on specific actions, from a behaviorist perspective, that were taken along the process leading toward success. Only if this step is applied well will the group's inquiry furnish a sound basis for producing actionable knowledge with implications for future activity.

Professionals often share a tendency, when describing what they do and especially when describing what they did, to couch their descriptions in concepts and models that are standard jargon in their fields. When attempting to generate actionable knowledge, such jargon tends to get in the way, as it enables practitioners to describe what they did in terms that do not actually reveal specific actions, such as "I built a trusting relationship with my students" or "I established an accepting atmosphere with my staff." By providing such descriptions, many professionals feel that they have indeed described what they did, but in fact, if one tries to imagine their specific behaviors, they remain very unclear and even confusing. Real-time authentic actions remain hidden behind such general descriptions. During group inquiry, professionals need to be prompted, and then repeatedly reminded, to let go of their familiar concepts and models while instead reconnecting with the *specific, detailed actions* that they actually applied (Rosenfeld et al., 2002). For example, to build a trusting relationship with her students, a teacher might explain that she spoke with students after school hours, announced that her class would go to a movie or concert together, ensured that students who didn't attend school would be contacted by her and other students, and so forth.

At this core step in the learning group's inquiry, the facilitator helps participants identify and mentally revisit the points identified in Step 5 as most fruitful for in-depth inquiry. Then, the group carefully reconstructs the details of the critical actions taken to achieve success by generating concrete, specific accounts of actions; the reasoning behind them; and their consequences (Rosenfeld et al., 2002) while avoiding any professional jargon that assumes common understanding while obscuring actual behavior. To revisit the junior high school with a violence problem described above, the following specific actions were identified as having been implemented at the key turning points as specific behaviors aiming to lower the school's aggression levels:

- Visits to students' homes by homeroom and other teachers (key turning points: conducting one-on-one relationships with students, recruiting relevant parties)

- Monthly discussions with parents in students' homes, particularly parents of children inclined to violence, on how to formulate a policy regarding violent students (key turning point: recruiting relevant parties)

- Noting occurrences of violence in students' personal files (key turning point: identifying aggressive subgroup)

- Encouraging students whose behavior has improved by praising them in front of other students and/or teachers and by awarding them symbolic prizes (key turning point: fostering transition from violent to responsible students)

As this example demonstrates, outlining a list of such concrete accounts of practitioners' specific actions that occurred at key turning points or milestones during the successful school enterprise, without lapsing back to the more familiar abstract and theoretical jargon typifying educational discourse, offers the learning group fertile ground for continuing its inquiry process.

STEP 7. CRAFT KEY PRINCIPLES
OF ACTION BASED ON SUCCESSFUL
ACTIONS SO OTHERS CAN LEARN FROM THEM

Principles of action are abstractions based on the details of each specific success story. They are formulated in a way that is general enough to be relevant to people in similar yet differing circumstances. Thus, the purpose of identifying action principles is to establish a common denominator for those actions that contributed to a given success in order for those actions to be applied in other settings (Sykes et al., 2006).

The major challenge at this step of the multistep inquiry format is to go beyond statements that are too abstract to be translated into actual practice. The key to the creation of appropriate action principles is to phrase them in a way that, on the one hand, is clearly anchored in specific actions but, on the other hand, is applicable to diverse future contexts. Phrasing the action principles in actionable language enables teachers to put these principles to future use under comparable and dissimilar circumstances alike, implementing them as a basis for learning and as possible venues for their own actions. For example, based on the aforementioned group's collective analysis of the junior high school that had succeeded in reducing incidents of violence such as harassment, assaults, cursing, and threats, the following recommended principles of actions were formulated by the group members:

- Delegating responsibility and positive assignments to students who are "troublemakers"

- Turning violent students into partners in formulating solutions to violence

- Turning parents into allies in the school's effort to contend with violence, both at the individual student level and at the school level

- Creating opportunities to collaboratively reflect on anti-violence values and endeavors

At the end of this step, the action principles phrased in actionable language comprise an important concrete resource for the school's future practical applications. As described later in this chapter, such principles require documentation and dissemination to maximize their impact. However, an additional step of the learning-from-success collaborative effort is needed—outlining some important issues for further inquiry.

STEP 8. IDENTIFY ISSUES FOR FURTHER STUDY

In this step of the multistep inquiry format, the learning facilitator should lead the group in taking a moment to explore possible additional issues related to the analyzed success that may be important to note, even if the group did not deem them to be critical for reconstructing the action strategies that made the success possible. Many such issues may have arisen during the collaborative inquiry process but were rejected in order to avoid sidetracking the inquiry away from drafting the final actionable principles of the analyzed success. Therefore, such issues may not have been explicitly factored into the group's inquiry process up to this step. Now, the facilitator and group members can raise them again in the context of summarizing issues requiring additional analysis by the practitioners who presented their success or even future exploration assigned to a different organizational forum. In the case of the junior high school facing student violence, for example, one issue that had been set aside was that since the implementation of the violence-targeting program that had been deemed successful, violence in the restrooms neither increased nor significantly decreased, and at this step of their inquiry process, the group decided to raise this issue for discussion at the school's general assembly.

This step is inherently linked with the open-ended nature of collaborative professional groups' learning. The recommended structured process of learning from success nevertheless allows for a great deal of open reflection on vague, ill-structured educational topics. Indeed, the ability to locate and cope with unresolved issues is a cornerstone of effective learning. Such issues may include various barriers, byproducts, difficulties, and disappointments—some subjective and others objective. Given the pessimism, stress, resistance, and insecurity that these may elicit, it is immensely important to expose group members to these issues within the context of the supportive collaborative learning group. Such exposure may foster practitioners' abilities to cope in real time with these issues and with their implications. Practice in coping with such issues sometimes enables practitioners to acquire skills for coping with increasingly challenging ill-structured issues or to take a step back in order to change the direction of action (Rosenfeld et al., 2002; Sykes et al., 2006). Thus, the identification of issues calling for additional study may also reveal a series of diverging paths leading to further individual and group learning.

STEP 9. EXPERIMENT AND DISSEMINATE

The ninth and final step of the format for inquiry into successful experiences/events comprises the need for both experimentation and dissemination. This step focuses on the collective learning forum's attempts to connect the knowledge that the group has gleaned—from the learning-from-success sessions—with actual classroom practices in their school. Highlighting the practical aspects of the collaborative learning process, this step aims to bridge the gap between verbal analysis of successes in the collective arena and actual implementation of learning in classrooms.

First, the collective learning group members attempt to experiment in their own classrooms with the actions pinpointed in the inquiry group in order to continue reflecting on and clarifying turning points, outcomes, costs, principles of action, and so forth. Teachers experiment with the new action-focused information in their own classrooms, thus acquiring additional information on which to reflect and then interpreting the acquired information, encoding it into memory, and acting on it further. As the information becomes more relevant to teachers' workplaces, reflections concerning teachers' experimentations are brought back to the collective learning forum for further analysis. Likewise, as teachers experiment with the information gleaned from the collective inquiry into successful practices, this information is endowed with explicit relevance within the specific school and then can finally be disseminated to all appropriate school contexts.

As an illustration of the experimentation and dissemination step, in a suburban high school that implemented a collective learning-from-success community toward the end of the year, the group decided that its members now needed to bridge the gap between their collective analysis of past professional success stories and those successes' practical implications in the school's classrooms (e.g., for teaching special education students in inclusive classes). The school's principal and superintendent (who was an equal participant in the development team sessions) emphasized the importance of this experimentation phase:

> We are approaching the end of the year. It is important to integrate the learning that emerged from the sessions with actions taken in the classrooms. Otherwise, we haven't done anything this year. We need to see the effect of the collective learning within classroom practices.
>
> —the high school principal

> I think that applying even one successful skill or pedagogical principle at the classroom level will clearly demonstrate that these sessions have a practical element, which will motivate teachers to learn together.
>
> —the school's superintendent

Hence, the group decided that, during this step, each participant in the learning forum would take one successful practice that had been analyzed during the year's sessions and try to implement it in real time within his or her actual classroom context. Participants were asked to report to the collective learning forum on their experimental implementation attempts so that the group could collectively reflect on these efforts. This method of experimenting in classrooms and then returning to discuss experiences in the collective learning sessions enabled participants to ask their colleagues for clarifications regarding the actions that had indeed led to the successes.

According to participants, in this experimentation phase, not only did they make attempts to connect the successes analyzed in the forum sessions with their own teaching practices within their classroom walls but teachers also perceived this step as an essential part of their learning process:

> I was confused until we started to implement the successes analyzed in the sessions. In this way, the information became more relevant to me and my colleagues.
>
> —a computer science teacher

Moreover, after experimentation in their own high school classrooms, teachers also began sharing these successful practices with colleagues in different subject areas outside the learning forum. This occurred without explicit prompting or a formal decision by the collective learning group, seemingly intensified following teachers' personal successful experimentation with the analyzed practices. Through such sharing encounters with peers, the forum's participants became ambassadors of the analyzed successes, thus enhancing dissemination processes in the school:

> In my subject area, my colleagues and I use successful practices that were analyzed during the learning-from-success sessions. We use successful strategies such as lowering students' anxiety levels before exams. At the beginning, when I shared these practices with my colleagues [who were not involved with the learning forum], they were very skeptical about using successful practices from other subject areas. After a while, some of them, during informal communication, commented that they had used these new practices in their classrooms.
>
> —a geography teacher

Interestingly, while the collective learning forum members experimented with successful practices in their classrooms and gradually shared analyzed success stories with their colleagues, another parallel sharing process emerged in this suburban high school:

> Participants also brought success stories [to the learning forum] from other staff members at the school who did not take part in the sessions and wanted help in learning what had led to their own successes.
>
> —the group's learning coordinator

This phenomenon of nonparticipating teachers turning to the professional learning community members in the school's hallways, asking for help in analyzing their own successes, appears to attest to the school's growing culture of collective learning from and dissemination of successful practices. From a systemic point of view, sharing their professional expertise with colleagues enabled teachers to clarify their unified professional strategies through a common language:

> Sharing the detailed actions that led to successful practices facilitated better use of the knowledge embedded within us, something we seldom do or know how to do. It widened the circle of learners and created a body of collective knowledge.
>
> —a history teacher

In order to capture this collective knowledge and disseminate it for optimal implementation in the school, at the end of this step, the group's learning coordinator assembled all the analyzed practices into a teaching kit, which was distributed to all faculty members. This was coupled with an invitation to the entire faculty to take part in a poster session in which learning forum participants presented their successful professional practices. At the end of this step (the end of the school year), teachers mainly focused on experimenting with the new practices in their own classes, although some also had a broader perspective on how to disseminate the learning-from-success process to other school staff as leverage for facilitating collective learning (Schechter, 2010).

This case illustration presented how one high school experimented with systematically analyzed success stories by applying them in various real-time classrooms and then how the school staff disseminated those successes based on hands-on familiarity with the ins and outs of the actions leading to success. This experimentation and dissemination step can be implemented in diverse ways by schools in different contexts. Each collective learning-from-success forum, guided by its school's particular needs and affordances, would do well to develop its own strategies for how best to implement experimentation and dissemination of successful pedagogical practices in order to maximize their embedment over time (see also the section later in this chapter, "D. The Production of Knowledge: Documentation for Dissemination").

BRIEF VERSION OF THE NINE-STEP INQUIRY PROCESS

The extended, systematic journey of collaborative learning from success, described above, requires prolonged engagement by school faculty members to analyze their own successes. Often, faculty members do not have this opportunity at their disposal, mainly during highly threatening and demanding circumstances, such as in systems facing the high-stakes standards that yield growing pressure for accountability, leaving little room or budget for long-term collaborative inquiry processes. Therefore, a short version of the learning-from-success inquiry format is needed, as in Table 4.1.

TABLE 4.1   Short Version of the Inquiry Format for Practitioners

I/we/they **succeeded in**				

Describe the situation *before*:		Describe the situation *after*:		

	Describe *turning points* along the road to success.		Pinpoint the *actions* taken at each turning point considered to be critical.		Formulate broad *principles of action* based on the analyzed success.
1.		→		→	
2.		→		→	
3.		→		→	
4.		→		→	
5.		→		→	
6.		→		→	

NOTE: Use concrete actionable language and avoid jargon or abstraction.

Identify **issues for further thought** and exploration:

Identify areas and settings for **experimentation**:

Identify strategies for **dissemination**:

SOURCE: Adapted from Ellenbogen-Frankovits et al., 2011

B. The Strategies Employed in the Learning-from-Success Inquiry Format

The second of the five different but complementary components comprising the learning-from-success journey refers to strategies. The collaborative learning group's facilitator may make use of four main strategies for designing and conducting the inquiry process in schools, all inherently intertwined with the multistep inquiry format described above (Sykes et al., 2006). As presented next, these four strategies pertain to maintaining focus on action to elicit tacit knowledge, adhering to the steps of inquiry, balancing macro and micro perspectives, and including diverse stakeholders into the learning process.

STRATEGY 1: FROM IMPLICIT KNOWLEDGE TO AN ACTION FORMAT

At the most basic level, to expose the tacit knowledge and action principles that contribute to success, collaborative group forums must uncover those concrete actions that were undertaken by the protagonists within the framework of the analyzed success story. To derive action principles from these stories, successes should be presented at the highest possible level of detail. When brought to light via action talk, this strategy often reveals practitioners' creative thinking and bold outside-the-box behavior. By encouraging such processes to unfold in the collective learning group, implicit knowledge is uncovered in an actionable way that focuses on the modalities of practice.

It is important for actions to be phrased in a descriptive, even dry manner that is not accompanied by explanations, generalizations, and interpretations. This strict attention to concise and descriptive wording makes it possible to focus solely on the action and to progress from it toward the derivation of action principles. This strategy is emphasized because explanations, especially at the beginning stages of the group inquiry, detract attention and time from the main activity leading to successful practice: learning about actions. Explanations originate in assumptions, beliefs, interpretations, and truths, thereby eliciting a tendency toward discussion that diverts attention from the major purpose of collective learning. This temptation must, of course, be overcome at the beginning stages of the inquiry process under the careful guidance of the group facilitator.

STRATEGY 2: ADHERENCE TO THE STEPS OF INQUIRY

The multistep format for collaborative inquiry (described above) provides safeguards, boundaries, and structure to enable the learning group to systematically conduct an efficient, judicious process of collective discourse and to achieve the desired outcomes within a reasonable amount of time. Especially when groups are large and heterogeneous, a collective forum can get unwieldy and messy; with a multitude of people come a multitude of opinions, perspectives, and experiences to be shared (Ellenbogen-Frankovits et al., 2011).

Sometimes different practitioners who were all involved in the same successful event under consideration may present the group with diverging accounts of that success story. To stay on-task, effective inquiry into a success story therefore often requires blocking some common types of professional conversation such as the theoretical underpinnings of actions or explanations of success or failure. For example, Step 6 requires the detailing of specific actions that were taken in or between turning points on the path to success. As it is often difficult for educators to reconstruct such actions, they frequently resort to general descriptions. During this step, persistence on the part of the facilitator to encourage speakers to view the success story solely from the action perspective is essential in order to enable practitioners to reconnect with the specific concrete actions that they previously performed. By means of this strategy of systematic adherence to the nine steps, the learning process develops layer upon layer, permitting the entire story's complexity—the total picture—to emerge little by little by presenting its parts as divided into areas that can be perceived discretely but that can also ultimately be joined into a whole.

STRATEGY 3: A MACRO → MICRO → MACRO PROGRESSION OF INQUIRY

How is it possible for an abbreviated process of inquiry to enable group members to fully benefit from their study of a complex long-term series of events? On one hand, learning from success is based on the assumption that every successful action is founded on implicit knowledge, which is apparent in the details of professional action (Rosenfeld et al., 2002). Significant learning therefore requires a detailed reconstruction of past professional actions. On the other hand, indiscriminate elaboration of detail can lead to a loss of direction and meaning, rendering the process lengthy and exhausting. Therefore, an important strategy for collective group inquiry into success stories is to merge macro and micro perspectives.

It is important to begin by introducing a macro view of the success in the first step of analysis, to outline the group's overall goals and motivate participants to embark on the inquiry process. This strategy might enhance the group's motivation to engage actively in this collective inquiry process, not only regarding the protagonists who are sharing their success story but also regarding their peers who are invited to discuss and analyze that story. Specifically, teachers might have low motivation due to concerns about the success story selected (they may think it's not of value to look at successes at all or that this particular story is not really a success) or they may have fears and misgivings about participating in the process itself (anxiety about their ability to analyze someone else's work intelligently or contribute meaningfully to group discourse, especially in front of the principal or other persons higher up in the school hierarchy). Hence, in the first step of analysis, the facilitator can allay concerns and fears and boost motivation related to this collective learning.

Next, in Steps 2–4, the inquiry format begins to zoom in, step by step, to examine the precursors and outcomes of the success story. At the core of the process, in Steps 5 and 6, the finest lens is used to carefully select the most important of micro actions underlying success for fine-grain analysis. Finally, the inquiry returns to the macro view, summarizing all the previous steps to formulate broader principles of action in Step 7, reviewing additional issues that accompanied the whole process but deserve further contemplation in Step 8 and then identifying avenues for experimentation and dissemination in Step 9. Returning to the macro level of discussion can help motivate and guide participants in translating their learning from success into future action (Sykes et al., 2006). Finding the balance between macro and micro perceptions is crucial—and is one of the learning coordinator's main roles (as discussed below).

STRATEGY 4: INCLUSION OF DIFFERENT ECHELONS IN THE LEARNING PROCESS

Involving representatives of diverse hierarchical levels in the learning-from-success process—such as supervisors, principals, mid-level managers, teachers, and students—helps accomplish another important goal beyond the main objective of transforming implicit knowledge to explicit knowledge by introducing action talk about successes. The collective learning process itself also aspires to change the normative discourse in a given organization or system. Engaging various stakeholders in an action learning strategy is meant to unsettle preconceived and stereotypical perceptions, thereby helping to unfreeze perceptions that were considered obvious or were taken for granted via abstract and generalized rhetoric. In other words, including different echelons in this collective learning process can reveal rich, multifaceted, actionable knowledge based on diverse perspectives.

C. Who Makes Up an Optimal Learning-From-Success Group?

The third of the five different but complementary components comprising the learning-from-success journey refers to the persons who comprise the collective learning group. The process of learning from success is based on reflection in a group setting that includes several partners. Importantly, although an individual can also undertake the process and arrive at certain understandings, it is preferable that it be conducted in a heterogeneous collective, encompassing different types of participants who can each contribute unique perspectives to enhance others' learning while also learning from them. All participants are invited to take an active part in the group, where learning-by-doing activity animates a process that allows participants to delve into different success stories.

In general, four types of participants take part in collective learning from success—the protagonist(s), facilitator, involved parties, and uninvolved interested parties—while an additional learning forum provides external support to this group. First and foremost, the *protagonist(s)* of the success story must be included in the collective learning group—the individual(s) who engaged in the successful enterprise. Second, the collaborative learning process requires a leader or guide—an inquiry *facilitator*. These two types of participants—the protagonist and the facilitator—comprise the basic dyad of inquirers, the minimum requirement for learning from success. As mentioned above, although it is possible to conduct a learning-from-success process through a one-on-one interview between protagonist and facilitator, there is considerable added value to the involvement of additional participants with various perspectives (Ellenbogen-Frankovits et al., 2011; Rosenfeld et al., 2002). Thus, optimally, the group should include not only people who were directly involved in the successful actions under examination (preferably with differing perspectives) but also interested parties who were not directly involved in the success story. Next, a more detailed description is presented of each of these types of participants in the learning group as well as a depiction of the leading forum, which offers external support to the inquiry facilitator.

THE PROTAGONIST(S): THE INDIVIDUAL(S) WHO ENGAGED IN A SUCCESSFUL ENTERPRISE

The success story that lies at the focus of the collective group inquiry should be shared firsthand by the practitioner—usually an individual but sometimes a pair of co-workers who partnered together to engage in or lead others to take the actions leading to success. For the learning process to be effective, this protagonist must have, alongside the ability to act successfully, the capacity to critically reflect upon his or her own practice, thinking back upon past actions. He or she needs to be able to respond to the facilitator's probing and directive questions non-defensively as well as to listen to peers' criticisms following self-disclosure by going beyond initial surface descriptions and progressively uncovering, reconstructing, and discovering aspects of his or her own actions and their effects upon relevant others. Similarly, he or she needs to be able to think critically of his or her own actions and their outcomes while demonstrating a willingness to recognize unseen negative effects and costs of those actions (Sykes et al., 2006).

THE LEARNING FACILITATOR/INQUIRY COORDINATOR

Although the inquiry coordinator may be a trained professional brought in from outside the school, by and large, he or she is usually someone inside the organization who is chosen by its leaders. The learning facilitator is well-versed in the realities of the organization, knows the team, and takes part in the school's main events. Overall, from an administrative and professional perspective, the coordinator's role goes beyond merely leading the actual learning-from-success sessions. That role includes the following:

1. Setting up regular times and places for the learning sessions

2. Identifying past successes in work with individuals or teams in the school that could lead to relevant material for joint study in the sessions

3. Leading the learning activity itself: Facilitating the learning-from-success sessions (sometimes on his or her own and at other times aided by a member of the learning group), which includes nurturing an open, responsive learning culture

4. Documenting the learning activity and disseminating the knowledge produced (formulated as principles of action) to participants and to a broader range of parties outside the sessions

With regard to leading the learning activity itself, the facilitator should perform a number of practices to create a learning ambiance that is simultaneously accepting and challenging while leaving ample space for participants' self-construction of actionable knowledge. Specifically, the learning-from-success facilitator should combine the following major tasks as part of his or her role. To *elicit an accepting learning climate*, the facilitator should (a) be committed to hearing the voices of all participants and to ensure that they are heard and considered and (b) be capable of seeing and connecting with participants' strengths and accomplishments. To *enhance adherence to the multistep format*, the facilitator should (a) preserve the general structure of the inquiry by insisting that the discussion remain focused and progress according to the inquiry steps (although being flexible to shift among steps if necessary) and (b) be capable of being very direct in facilitation, actively blocking lines of inquiry that are likely to be unproductive and restrict a learning culture. To *foster the transition from implicit knowledge to an action format*, the facilitator should (a) encourage action talk rather than abstract and jargon expressions; (b) make implicit knowledge explicit by asking for clarifications, especially in the context of concrete actions; and (c) conceptualize what has been said by relating it to concepts that are familiar to participants. To *balance macro and micro perceptions*, the facilitator should reflect back with participants about where they are in the inquiry process and keep them aware of its progression.

While leading the learning activity itself, the learning facilitator must serve as a gatekeeper who alerts participants in the learning community to a priori professional schematic models and principles of action. The learning facilitator needs to abstain from conveying unequivocal statements, which may hinder the formation of a constructive dialogue among faculty members. Especially at the inception stages of a professional learning community focused on teachers' successes, it is important that the learning facilitator encourage participants to share their opinions. Learning facilitators who impose their own thoughts, rather than helping staff members to transform their ambitions and hopes into shared principles of action, will only strengthen teachers' dependency on the facilitator while closing off opportunities for genuine collective learning from success.

Overall, a major role of the inquiry coordinator during the collective learning sessions is to work toward leading an open, safe learning-from-success culture. Effective reflexive spaces in school are contingent on the learning facilitator's role in promoting a culture of inquiry, openness, and trust. The learning leader must facilitate the openness of school learning communities by conveying the diverse dreams, hopes, and ambitions of staff members, embracing the metaphor of looking through a kaleidoscope (Hargreaves & Fullan, 2012). Thus, through modeling and explanation, the learning facilitator must convey to group members that the point of collaborative learning is neither a political debate nor the manipulation of people to support a cause. There are no "right answers" or "right paths" to success. The learning facilitator must protect staff members from power games while nurturing the skills of listening, inquiring, and reflecting.

Similarly, in order for learning facilitators to strengthen the social processes involved in collective learning, it is imperative to cultivate discourse communities that are based on mutual respect and the joint responsibility to freely share and explore staff members' successes. In these discourse communities, members share their expertise based on free-flowing and safe dialogic means for fostering new and creative approaches to school needs. To this end, learning facilitators need to create a safe practice field where multiple professional successes are crystallized.

As part of facilitating the learning-from-success sessions, inquiry coordinators should work toward nurturing a culture of openness by encouraging a safe space for teachers to expose their tacit assumptions in the collective arena of learning from success. Hence, inquiry coordinators must develop an atmosphere of generosity and acceptance in the learning group. They need to create a forthcoming environment prior to and during the inquiry into teachers' own successes. Reflecting on personal beliefs and values during the learning-from-success process can, in itself, help to facilitate a culture of openness and to enhance teachers' commitment and passion toward this collective inquiry. It is imperative to create spaces where practitioners can feel protected from insults, deprecation, or disapproval when sharing their perceived professional expertise and strengths as a means of improving pedagogical practices. The leadership challenge is to reduce the impact of defensive routines that guide people's behavior (Argyris & Schon, 1996) by expressing patience and empathy and constructing a bridge between different group members' positions.

This "leadership bridge" is especially important when it comes to defining what the group agrees should be considered a success in the collective learning arena. It is well known that teachers do not necessarily share the same beliefs and values about what is successful or not; thus, one teacher's perceived success may be another's perceived failure. When participants classify their colleagues' experiences into either successful or unsuccessful categories, learning leaders can uncover the potentially rich information residing within each experience. In order to cope with the unintended division between "successful" and "unsuccessful" teachers, learning facilitators can serve as gatekeepers for any dispositional ideology while empowering teachers to authentically share what they perceive as their successful practices. It is important that learning facilitators remain open to lessons learned from the collective endeavor without being too bound by rigid hierarchical rules. In other words, they can encourage teachers to inquire into their successful practices, acknowledging faculty members as creative partners in a joint learning venture.

The case of an urban high school inquiry facilitator may illustrate some ideas for how learning coordinators can begin to promote a culture of openness and trust in initiating collective learning from success (Schechter, 2010). On the verge of launching a collective learning-from-success endeavor in her school, this facilitator was aware, through informal conversations, that several future participants were skeptical about the possible contribution of the upcoming learning-from-success sessions. In light of this skepticism, the facilitator devoted the first month (two sessions) of the collective learning group mainly to building a learning culture based on mutual trust and dialogue. To achieve this safe climate, the learning coordinator started the process of learning from success by initiating collective inquiry into successful pedagogical practices that were removed from the specific school context rather than beginning with successful experiences by a protagonist from within the school. For instance, during the second session, the learning coordinator showed clips from the film, *Stand and Deliver* (Musca & Menendez, 1988), with the aim of facilitating collective reflection with regard to the math teacher's detailed actions that led to his success in teaching undisciplined, unmotivated high school students. The coordinator then invited teachers to share successes in small groups of three. At the end of the session, she explained to the whole group:

> We started in groups of three because, in this way, everyone has a voice, and it is much easier to open up. Today, it was too early to reflect on our own successes in the whole forum. We will analyze professional successes in the whole forum in our next session.

The learning coordinator coupled this approach during the sessions with private conversations outside the sessions with the aforementioned skeptical teachers to address their concerns and offer personalized explanations about the potential of collective learning from success to bolster teachers' professional development. Thus, the first stage of invitation and framework-building focused on inquiring into more peripheral successes that did not considerably affect ongoing school practices. Inasmuch as teachers encounter difficulties learning with and from their colleagues, the first two sessions dealt with successes that were removed from core school practices in order to develop the necessary culture and cognitive readiness required for inquiry into the teachers' own professional successes. Therefore, even when inquiring into successes, an invitation and framework-building stage is important in creating a forthcoming environment prior to the inquiry into participants' own successes, thus recognizing defensive routines (Argyris & Schon, 1996) during the organizational social learning endeavor.

OTHERS INVOLVED IN OR AFFECTED BY THE PROFESSIONAL PRACTICES

In the context of successful practices, those involved in a success story may be colleagues within or across organizations or they may be individuals who are hierarchically related to the person whose actions are being studied. The learning-from-success group should include parties in the learning process such as collaborators, subordinates/superiors, team members, or recipients of the successful outcomes. The assessment of these outcomes and of the processes that produced them is necessarily incomplete without the active voice and involvement of these practitioners. Integrating the perspectives of several individuals who each have a different viewpoint on the same subject of study makes it possible to form a more holistic picture of the action, its effects, and its perceived significance (Sykes et al., 2006).

In particular, the beneficiaries of successful actions, such as school students, are often sought out and included in the inquiry. This is based on the assumption that education organizations can only be successful in their practices if they produce positive outcomes for their students within the community they serve.

INTERESTED UNINVOLVED COLLEAGUES

Colleagues who have an interest in the general area of activity being analyzed but who were not directly involved in the specific actions comprising the success story (e.g., professionals from another school, members of the same staff who did not participate in the analyzed project) add important perspectives to the learning process. Often, people who were involved in a challenging action, even one with beneficial products, are so mired in their dilemmas that they find it difficult to see the successful actions. Moreover, even if they recognize that they have succeeded, it may be difficult for them to perceive the value embedded in their success that can justify others' learning from it. Colleagues introduce a more holistic perspective into the learning process, which can reveal the value of an action to those who performed it. Their recognition and respect can help those involved in the action under scrutiny to see themselves in a more favorable light and from a broader perspective.

No less important than what they contribute, colleagues automatically extrapolate from the actions being studied to similar fields and different contexts, given their simultaneous proximity to and distance from the actions. While the group is focusing aloud on one case, they are mentally actively learning about their own cases. This "reflection–conversation" process (Grimmett, 1988) creates a dialogue between the cognitive frameworks shared by practitioners based on information in their practice setting and colleagues' own existing mental frameworks in their unique school contexts (Schechter, 2012). For example, they may ask themselves in which situations certain activities are or are not relevant to their work due to differences in circumstances. In other words, the group participants are continually internally pondering the question, *What are the limitations on the use of the knowledge I have just gained?* By comparing what they are learning to their own work, they help inculcate success into a broader area of activity (Sykes et al., 2006).

Finally, these participants in the learning process potentially become disseminators of this mode of learning to their own contexts, thereby expanding the potential impact of the inquiry far beyond the boundaries of the specific forum in which it took place. Through them, the actions and principles of action that underlie success in a particular endeavor can be disseminated to related fields of practice, organizational structure, policy, research and evaluation, and training (Rosenfeld et al., 2002).

THE LEADING FORUM (EXTERNAL TO THE COLLECTIVE LEARNING GROUP)

Altogether, the learning coordinator shapes the group's learning process, inculcates it, and takes responsibility for its continuity. To be effective in this position, however, the coordinator cannot operate in a vacuum in the school. An optimal learning-from-success process is supported by a permanent leading forum that operates in the school.

A school's leading forum is a permanent small forum comprised of the leading individuals in the school, such as the principal, the school's superintendent, and the learning coordinator. This forum meets regularly to steer, shape, advise, and evaluate the learning processes occurring in the long-term series of learning-from-success sessions. Beyond contributing to a school culture that supports learning from success, the school leaders in this leading forum also create the necessary institutionalized arrangements for collaborative learning by allocating time, space, and resources. The leading forum is also responsible for suggesting possible avenues for integrating the learning group's principles of action into day-to-day school life

(Schechter et al., 2008). The following are some recommended design issues to be contemplated by the leading forum:

- How can we cope with opposition or resistance among the staff?

- How can we link learning from success to core school issues?

- How can we create a learning experience of a different kind?

- How can we cope with the staff's sense of burnout regarding professional development training programs?

- What is the place of the principal in this collective learning process?

- How can we implement the learning-from-success format when the learning coordinator is still learning?

- How can the learning forum members experiment with successful practices in their classrooms? How can learners connect the knowledge that the group has gleaned from the collective inquiry into successful practices with actual classroom practices?

- How can we disseminate learning-from-success principles of action beyond the participants in the learning forum itself?

- How can we expand the learning-from-success forum to other circles of participants (students, parents, other teachers)?

D. THE PRODUCTION OF KNOWLEDGE: DOCUMENTATION FOR DISSEMINATION

The fourth of the five different but complementary components comprising the learning-from-success journey refers to its products. The learning coordinator is responsible for the documentation of every learning encounter; a person may be appointed for this purpose or group participants may take turns performing this task. This documentation records the minutes of each session, trying to detail the contents expressed by participants with the greatest accuracy possible. The initial documentation is then summarized clearly and concisely to capture its main contents and then is distributed to participants. In a shared document, the participants are asked to add more action talk and principles of action, if necessary. The accumulated documentation serves as raw material for the identification of action principles on which future practices may be based. Thus, documenting knowledge acquired from the group inquiry process enables it to be retained and disseminated for use in other contexts, thereby providing the basis for successful future action.

The documentation format is structured to meet the needs of people who want to use the knowledge produced through learning from success. It enables various stakeholders to determine whether the subject is relevant and interesting to them, whether the context is similar to their own, and whether this particular success story is worthy of learning. It helps them identify specific actions that contributed to positive outcomes and determine which ones they might use in their own work (Rosenfeld et al., 2002; Sykes et al., 2006). For example, a document reporting actionable principles from a grade-level social intervention that was successful for eighth graders can be shared with all the other grade-level coordinators or a document on successful teamwork practices from the English language coordinator can be disseminated to all subject-matter coordinators. Sharing of such documents could be accompanied by a one-time presentation of the project at a management meeting to optimize its likelihood of generalizability. Likewise, some documents may be relevant to the entire teacher body in a school, such as those regarding means for reducing student aggression. In those cases, documents could be disseminated using the school's digital teacher forums via social media or the school website, accompanied by the principal's instructions on changes in school policy. For documents that have wider implications across schools, governmental or local education superintendents may be appropriate recipients, and they may be invited to meet with the learning-from-success group to deepen understanding and better contextualize the written documentation.

E. EVALUATION

The last of the five different but complementary components comprising the learning-from-success journey refers to evaluation of the school's collaborative group process of learning from success. This evaluation should be conducted each time a successful story's analysis is completed, with follow-up after a period of time to evaluate later impact.

Evaluation comprises three levels of assessment: the individual level, the group level, and the school level (Sykes et al., 2006). At the individual level, each group member evaluates his or her own needs by asking a series of questions:

- Is the context in which the analyzed success took place similar to my context? (focusing on relevant contexts)

- What activities were performed to reach success, and which of them might I consider in my own work? (focusing on turning points, essential activities, and principles of action)

- What else would be interesting to know about what transpired? (focusing on unanticipated by-products)

- Should I learn more about these activities? (focusing on additional information and unresolved issues)

- To what extent did I actively contribute to the group discourse? To what extent did I overcome my inhibitions and concerns in order to share my experiences and opinions with the group? How can I work to improve my self-disclosure capacity? What was I able to teach my peers? (focusing on the group's learning culture and reciprocity)

At the group level, group members should conduct a collective evaluation regarding the group's internal and external effectiveness: namely, how the group itself functioned and what impact the group's processes and products may have had on the wider system, respectively (Sykes et al., 2006). The following may serve as a sample tentative outline for evaluating the group's process of collaborative learning from success in schools:

A. Evaluation of the group's internal functioning, to be conducted each time a successful story's analysis is completed:
    i. Did the collective learning group identify success in selected areas of the school's work?
    ii. Did the collective learning group develop principles of action that effectively contributed to the student, classroom, grade level, school, and/or community?
    iii. Did the collective learning group document that success in actionable terms?
    iv. Did the collective learning group provide a safe space for members to divulge thoughts and actions?

B. Evaluation of the group's external impact, to be conducted at a follow-up interval after a period of time:
    i. Did the school put practices and structures into operation based on the principles of action generated during the group's learning-from-success journey regarding that specific analyzed success?
    ii. Did the collective learning group help promote a school culture of documentation that supports the production and eventual dissemination of learning?
    iii. Did the collective learning group contribute to the school's continued development and institutionalization of mechanisms and opportunities that allow for in-school collective learning for stakeholders who work within the system?

Finally, the school's permanent leading forum should conduct formative evaluation based on the above questions. Together, the school leaders (such as the principal, superintendent, and facilitator) can evaluate each success story's effectiveness at the school level, which can help them strategize about the long-term collective process of learning from success.

In sum, this chapter has presented the main components of a journey into professional successes as an impetus to schoolwide learning and positive change. This inquiry process is based on a structured study tool, guided group discussion, documentation, and evaluation (Ellenbogen-Frankovits et al., 2011; Sykes et al., 2006). The collaborative inquiry of learning from success is meant to reveal the hidden knowledge that contributed to success, so that it can be used in the future (Schechter et al., 2008). It should be stressed, however, that using this inquiry process in schools is far from a technical process. Two major characteristics of the inquiry—its ability to uncover the richness of professional knowledge underlying successful actions and its engagement of stakeholders from a variety of backgrounds in a joint learning venture—enable this inquiry to provide the impetus for a significant change in awareness and in the nature of the discourse regarding educators' wisdom of practice.

CHAPTER 5

The National Program for Learning From Success in Schools

This program had joint learning with colleagues, mutual encouragement (which is very important), getting to know other teachers and how they teach and cope with situations . . . getting to know a variety of teaching methods. . . . The atmosphere was positive, which produced positive energies. In the past, we always focused on the negative and did not see what actually does work. . . . Through the program of learning from success, we began to focus on what is successful. . . . We began to check [on] what is actually going on in our school and to analyze our successes together.

—a high school math teacher

Strengthening positive points and learning from successful processes can be no less meaningful and effective than learning from failures. . . . It is very important to bring success stories to the forefront and learn from them. This is also a great way to give the stage to people who don't always get an opportunity to express themselves, and it is also important for a system like a school that doesn't always reward those who deserve it. . . . Putting a spotlight on people for good things that they do and learning from these experiences is so enriching. . . . The connection between teachers is strengthened. . . . Another benefit from the process is that professional teachers have created very good relationships with homeroom teachers and this has improved the formers' status.

—a high school principal

We have gone from being a group of teachers who "put out fires," so to speak (that is, just coping with the most urgent occurrences and [trying] to keep up), to a group that learns, contemplates, and plans while also enjoying this collective learning. The program has led to an improvement in student achievements and classroom atmosphere in general.

—a ninth-grade coordinator

Widespread implementation of learning from success, as a habit of practice that is consistently applied across numerous schools simultaneously, requires policy intervention on a larger scale. This chapter presents a comprehensive example of such an initiative as enacted at the national level to design and implement an innovative program, Learning from Success as Leverage for Schoolwide Learning, while illustrating possible applications of the program in three diverse participating schools. This program (see Schechter, Sykes, & Rosenfeld, 2008) was the initiative of the Department of Secondary Education in the Israeli Ministry of Education in collaboration with the Unit for Learning from Success of the Myers-JDC-Brookdale Institute, an applied research institute on social policy and human services. According to the Gini coefficient for measuring a nation's distributive inequality, Israel is among the Western countries with the broadest gap between rich and poor, alongside the United States and the United Kingdom, experiencing great diversity among school populations and a wide gap in students' achievement distributions (Organization for Economic Co-operation and Development, 2016).

The goal of this national program was to integrate learning from success into ongoing school processes and structures of 20 participating middle and secondary schools, with the express purpose of stimulating ongoing collective professional learning. Participating schools expressed interest in systematically implementing collaborative learning from success in their schools. Based on the conceptual discussion appearing in Chapter 2, the major rationales of the national program were threefold:

1. The expertise of educational practitioners in schools is a rich, barely tapped resource.

2. Due to systemic bias toward learning from difficulties or failures, successes in schools have rarely been the object of deliberate collective learning.

3. For the expertise that underlies success to be tapped, it must undergo a process (learning from success) through which educators' tacit knowledge is transformed into school knowledge, thus assisting faculty members in verifying, sorting, and filtering data.

THE COLLECTIVE WISDOM OF PRACTICE

THE NATIONAL PROGRAM'S GOALS

Based on these main rationales for the national program, its major goals were formulated as follows: (a) to impart school staff members with the learning-from-success skills that would enable them to make a significant contribution to the production of knowledge that could advance their students and (b) to see *learning from success* as a means of promoting learning in schools by serving as a catalyst for ongoing learning and thus for realization of their school mission.

This national program marked the first time that learning from success was integrated into ongoing organizational processes and structures. To make this possible, learning from success was systematized into learning formats as well as documentation formats, which structured both the work and the language of school personnel participating in the program. Each school decided which areas or issues would be the focus of its learning. It did so while keeping in mind the program's objective of being "result-oriented," namely, of improving outcomes in chosen areas of learning (Ellenbogen-Frankovits, Shemer, & Rosenfeld, 2011; Schechter et al., 2008), although the national program was not tied to any specific national standards. Table 5.1 presents the expected shift from primarily learning from problems and obstacles toward a more reciprocal learning process focused on practitioners' own successful and satisfactory professional practices.

Beyond the stated goals of the national program as devised by its initiators, it emerged that the school principals on the ground also expected this program to serve another goal: to render a sociocultural impact on schools in disadvantaged or peripheral areas of the country. Among the 20 participating middle and secondary schools, one fourth represented minorities—three schools in the Muslim sector and two schools in the Christian sector, with the remaining 15 schools in the Jewish majority sector. Moreover, 40% of the participating schools (eight schools) were located in rural areas around the country (with the remaining 12 schools in urban

TABLE 5.1   The Expected Shifts in Schools' Learning Processes

SCHOOL DOMAIN	SHIFT FROM	SHIFT TOWARD
Staff's self-efficacy	Discouraged, focused on learning from obstacles	Sense of ability to learn from successes and contribute to colleagues' learning
Plasticity of learning processes	Stagnant	Dynamic
Flexibility of paradigms	Fixed working paradigms	Openness to learning and exploring alternative paradigms
Culture	Lack of a culture that promotes sharing, fear of exposure and criticism	Readiness to share, excitement about sharing, atmosphere of reciprocal generosity

centers). Whereas most urban schools participating in this program were located in relatively high-level socioeconomic environments, most schools from the rural environments (including the Muslim and Christian schools) were in a constant struggle to provide their students with "good enough" education in their low-level socioeconomic environments. Therefore, the learning-from-success program was perceived, especially by the principals of schools located in rural areas, as a possible savior for these struggling schools. Put differently, practitioners from rural low-level socioeconomic environments perceived the intentional focus on successes within their schools as an opportunity to alter their students' and staff members' long-term sense of stagnation and preoccupation with problems and failures.

PROGRAM DEVELOPMENT TEAMS AND CIRCLES OF LEARNERS

At each school, the national program was carried out by both a *development team* and a *circle of learners*. The development team was comprised of the school principal, a learning coordinator (a senior staff member chosen to lead the program), and the school's regional superintendent, along with a learning companion from the national development team (from the Ministry of Education) who served as a reflective/critical partner for each participating school. This leading forum met about once every four weeks with the school's circle of learners to follow up on developments.

Each school's circle of learners, typically comprising between 10 to 15 participants, was a learning forum that met regularly, usually scheduled after regular teaching hours, under organization and facilitation by the school's learning coordinator. In this forum, both teachers and administrators took an active role, with no participation of outside members (e.g., the learning companion). To support the 20 learning coordinators in organizing and facilitating this learning forum, they were provided with 28 hours of off-site training.

The circle of learners was self-directed by its participants and oriented toward addressing issues at the heart of the school's vision and development process. Learning in a school's circle of learners included the following aspects: (1) holding regularly scheduled learning workshops, (2) identifying and analyzing successful school practices, (3) documenting the learning process, (4) identifying effective modes of collective learning, and (5) disseminating the methodology and products of learning from success to other schools' learning forums.

The program incorporated two components within each workshop conducted by the circle of learners: learning from success and learning about learning. The main part of each session was devoted to learning from success, where the school's learning coordinator facilitated the learning group's identification of staff's and students' successes, coordination of structured group inquiries into the actions that contributed to these successes, and documentation of the processes and products of these inquiries. In other words, in this uniquely designed learning forum, educators reflected upon school successes, discovering and explicating the tacit knowledge that led to those successes and formulating them in actionable terms as a basis for their dissemination.

The second component within each workshop conducted by the circle of learners was devoted to learning about learning ("deutero-learning" as described by Bateson, 1972). Toward the end of each session (approximately the last 15 minutes), participants were encouraged to reflect on how they had learned together during the collective inquiry into successful practices (the first component of the session: learning from success). Participants were asked to jointly ponder the way in which they had communicated in the collective arena. Learning about learning focuses on questions such as *What is our preferred learning style? What specific procedures did we use today that helped us achieve meaningful learning?* and *How can we learn better as a group?* Other examples of such learning include the contribution of structured inquiry and documentation formats to practitioners' ability to express their own capacities to focus on successes, to deepen their own learning, and to understand the different tempos and pathways of collective learning. Thus, throughout the year, participants explicitly reflected on their real-time processes of collective learning in order to generate insights about productive collective learning methods and procedures.

THE LEARNING-FROM-SUCCESS INQUIRY FORMAT

The comprehensive learning-from-success inquiry format described in Chapter 4 had barely been formulated during the initiation phase of this national program. At that time, learning from success was still more of an approach and an ethical stance than an actual multistep inquiry model. To serve as guidelines for the 20 schools, therefore, a preliminary model was developed, comprising a series of unelaborated headings. This preliminary model was shared with principals, learning coordinators, learning companions, and participants in the circle of learners in order to assess its suitability for school contexts. Thus, the inquiry format was fine-tuned through an ongoing feedback process together with the program's own participants.

The national program's learning-from-success inquiry format, which was later developed into the full multistep format discussed in Chapter 4, was originally designed with the intention of revealing the hidden knowledge that had contributed to successful practices. As practitioners tend to use general descriptions when reconstructing their past successful practices, it was important to structure the inquiry format in a way that would capture the specific actions that had been taken along the usually complex path to success. Therefore, persistence in viewing the success from an action perspective was essential in enabling teachers to reconnect with what they had done. The learning coordinators were instructed to use the inquiry format carefully in order to develop practitioners' reconstruction, layer upon layer, before ultimately joining them all into a whole.

The following stages of the learning-from-success format were used by the 20 schools as a sort of road map to depict group learning that deals with complex past successful endeavors. The inquiry format used by participating schools consisted of seven steps:

1. *Identify a success that is worthy of study*: Briefly describe a few success stories and tentatively choose one of them for joint investigation. A success is considered worthy of group study when it offers a definite benefit to student outcomes, which is traceable to deliberate professional actions. This benefit needs to be aligned with the school's objectives.

2. *Succinctly describe the success in terms of* before *and* after: Provide a concise description of the relevant situation before and after the endeavor was undertaken. Generating these two descriptions and highlighting the positive changes in the situation can suggest to the group that successful actions have indeed taken place.

3. *Describe the positive outcomes*: Reflect more deeply and critically on how the success is defined. Expanding and deepening investigation into the successful outcomes can help the group construct a clear picture of the nature of the change that has taken place.

4. *Describe negative consequences and costs*: Consider the negative consequences of having achieved the change described in the earlier steps. The quality and value of past success as a basis for group learning can only be determined by rigorously weighing positive and negative outcomes as well as costs.

5. *Identify critical turning points or milestones on the path to success*: Choose critical turning points and reconstruct the concrete actions that led to the successful outcomes. With the facilitator's help, break the successful occurrence down into chronologically ordered stages marked by turning points and/or key milestones. This stage may be seen as the heart of the inquiry format, when people who participated in the successful endeavor reconstruct the details of those events and actions that were crucial to its achievement. It is within this detail that the treasures of the process may be discovered.

6. *Craft tentative key principles of action based on the successful actions*: Develop *principles of action*, which are abstractions based on the details of each specific success story. They should be general enough so that they can be applicable to other educational contexts.

7. *Identify issues for further inquiry*: Generate and consider issues for further study. Inviting and noting such issues assures the open-ended nature of the learning session.

ANALYTIC METHODS TO EVALUATE THE PROGRAM'S IMPLEMENTATION

Qualitative data were collected throughout the program's first year of implementation (Schechter et al., 2008). Participants were provided with an evaluation form aimed at assessing the collective learning process and its products. More specifically, participants were asked about the effects of the program as well as the impediments they encountered throughout the process. Altogether, the 20 participating schools yielded 145 evaluation forms for analysis (with a minimum of five forms per school). These participants varied in line with the schools' diversity of practitioners participating in their learning-from-success workshops. The learning forums that developed in the schools often comprised a heterogeneous group, whether involving school administrators, homeroom teachers, subject coordinators, grade-level coordinators, or teachers of remedial classes.

The following are examples of questions appearing on the form:

- What were your thoughts and feelings before the first session?

- What were your thoughts and feelings at the beginning phase of the collective learning-from-success practices?

- Can you identify impediments to this collective learning?

- Do you think the workshops had costs or negative results? If so, what were they?

- Do you feel that this collective learning contributed to your professional knowledge?

- Did the collective learning within the circle of learners have any impact on your school's climate?

- How could the workshops be improved to create better joint learning?

Overall, the evaluation forms revealed three major domains for successes that the circle of learners had studied over the first year of the program. The participating schools had focused on the following main areas of success: (1) improving the achievements of poorly performing students (e.g., students from a remedial class had succeeded in mathematics, students from remedial classes had passed matriculation exams), (2) improving instruction (e.g., successes in teaching complex concepts, successes of children with special needs in inclusive classes, development of innovative teaching tools), and (3) improving coping with discipline and violence problems (e.g., successes in responding to incidents of vandalism, turning "troublemakers" into students with roles and responsibilities, developing an engaging learning climate in the classroom). Additional areas of success beyond these major domains included school-based entrepreneurial ventures and the development of effective teamwork among staff that later contributed to student achievements.

Analysis of the program's first year of implementation via qualitative formative evaluation by its participants yielded data on the impediments to the program's effectiveness and on the program's effects. Following the presentation of these two sets of findings, case studies from three participating schools are presented to elucidate how the learning-from-success journey can be undertaken in diverse settings.

IMPEDIMENTS TO THE COLLECTIVE PROCESS OF LEARNING FROM SUCCESS

The initial program stages, where schools became acquainted with the program and explored ways to implement it, were fraught with difficulties. At the opening meetings, participants expressed concerns regarding the recommended changes in thinking—the shift from problems to successes and the focus on collective learning—that might accompany the program's implementation in their schools. These difficulties related to the "concessions" that the teams realized they would have to make if they were to jointly explore their successes. The initial concerns focused mainly on four issues, as follows.

IS IT LEGITIMATE TO DISCUSS ONE'S SUCCESSES?

The issue of legitimacy for success-focused learning was a prominent one, voiced by many of the learning coordinators:

> The school's organizational culture doesn't speak in a language of learning from successes. It's not easy to change our way of thinking from focusing on failure to focusing on success as a catalyst for team learning; we're used to analyzing problems.
>
> —a high school English teacher

> I saw this as a potentially helpful tool. First, it could help us understand the meaning of successes, because we're constantly talking about what isn't good, about failures . . . that's the innovation here. It takes time for a school to absorb this. You're putting something completely new and optimistic in front of us. The idea that is especially incredible is that you have hidden knowledge here, and you're invited to use it, contrary to what teachers are accustomed to thinking.
>
> —a high school geography teacher

At the start of the program, it was clearly evident that participants were more comfortable looking for their difficulties than analyzing their successes in the presence of their colleagues. Teachers pointed to their own tendency to learn from their failed practices:

> It's easier to find faults and failures and to try to solve them. It's much harder to acknowledge your success in the presence of your colleagues.
>
> —a middle school math teacher

> It was an interesting process because you'd expect people would find it easy to connect to successes . . . but actually it was very difficult for them to talk about it. . . . What bothered the team was a feeling that if we relate only to successes, we might not be able to deal with the painful issues.
>
> —a high school history teacher

Teachers noted that, before initiating the national program, they generally would meet to solve problems, and in these meetings, their professional successes were usually not collectively explored. Gradually, it became evident that in most schools, a lack of openness had prevented teachers from presenting their professional successes to their colleagues. Interestingly, an English teacher stated that "some teachers considered exposing their successes in the learning forum as an act of arrogance." Similarly, there was a common fear that by publicly displaying one's successes, one would run the risk of arousing potentially destructive jealousy among others.

WAS IT REALLY A SUCCESS?

Teachers did not necessarily share the same beliefs and values about what could be considered a successful professional practice; thus, one teacher's perceived success could be another's perceived failure:

> Only a few teachers who presented their successful work managed to convince me that we can recognize their experiences as successful and subsequently learn from them.
>
> —a high school English teacher

> Because of a lack of innovativeness, there were almost no successful practices that I could directly apply in my own work.
>
> —a middle school chemistry teacher

These perceptions may have been raised because teachers compared their colleagues' successes to their own professional standards:

> Not everyone likes to talk about themselves and their successes and to share them with others. Personally, I have no problem giving out my materials, but there are teachers who have a problem with it. . . . Maybe my success will not be seen as such by others, and maybe I don't meet their standards. . . . Some teachers were afraid of this.
>
> —a high school biology teacher

Although the purpose of learning from success was to create a learning community, several teachers classified their colleagues' experiences as either successful or unsuccessful right from the onset of each inquiry, thus foregoing the possibility of learning from the potentially rich information embodied within the process of analyzing each experience.

WAS IT SUCCESSFUL BECAUSE OF MY ACTIONS?

In many instances, participants attempted to quickly explain the end results of their successes rather than engaging in a process of detecting the specific actions leading to them; however, action specificity is the essence of the learning-from-success inquiry format. This common tendency to avoid critical reflection can be explained as stemming from a competitive atmosphere.

> There was a sense of competitiveness—who succeeded more and who will impress the audience.
>
> —a high school literature teacher

> The atmosphere in the learning-from-success forum induced a sense of competitiveness, which divided the participants into two main groups: teachers who were successful and others who were not. This unintended division influenced participants to use general terms when asked to describe the actions leading to their successes.
>
> —a middle school learning coordinator

As a result of this division, some participants tried to avoid the tedious job of delving into detailed inquiry into their actions that had led to success because it presented a potential threat to the validity of their successes. Moreover, teachers were reluctant to delve into concrete actions leading to success because they wondered whether their successes might have evolved through luck or coincidence rather than through their own planned actions:

> I was hesitant to reveal my successes because they might have occurred as a result of a mere coincidence and not been directly caused by my actions.
>
> —a high school art teacher

Thus, practitioners were reluctant to inquire into successful practices because of the possibly loose connections between their actions and the successful results.

WAS THIS COLLECTIVE LEARNING FROM SUCCESS JUST ANOTHER PROJECT ON MY TO-DO LIST?

As teachers face an endless stream of new projects, curricular reforms, and top-down policy changes, many of the participants in these collective learning-from-success forums perceived the program as just another project on their to-do list. They emphasized that the program constituted an enormous burden on their daily work. The data suggested that scarcity of time and space hindered schools' attempts to implement the program. This resulted in excessive pressure upon teachers:

> The teachers didn't cooperate. The system is full of bureaucratic issues to be dealt with, which didn't allow the teachers to focus on one topic and study it deeply. This was very stressful. The question was how to squeeze it all in. I approached many teachers about it, but they always complained that they didn't have time. It just faded away because we had too many projects already, and no time.
>
> —a high school learning coordinator

Hence, having too many projects and having too little time were considered problems that led teachers to fail in implementing the learning-from-success program:

> I don't know how to motivate the staff to get involved in the process and commit to it while at the same time they're loaded with projects and a thousand other things because you need to accomplish this, that, and the other, and there's just no end to it.
>
> —a middle school learning coordinator

> We were flooded with so many things and eventually [we] didn't do anything as required.
>
> —a middle school counselor

> There was a terrible feeling: Here comes another commitment, another workload. The main difficulty was that there was no opportunity to delve into collective learning from success. We had good intentions, wishing to give it the attention it deserved, but we couldn't. Our daily schedule was not suited for it.
>
> —a high school math coordinator

The data also suggested that no special attention was given to the program on the school agenda:

> I don't understand why the school didn't set a specific time for the program. During the usual discussions about pupils' achievements, report cards, discipline problems, and trip planning, we found a few minutes to discuss it. It just got "swallowed up" among other things. The program was not monitored as it should have been, and the staff didn't receive ongoing support.
>
> —a middle school biology teacher

The teachers stated that they had neither the time nor the necessary support to sustain collective learning from success. Consequently, they felt overloaded with the introduction of the program into their daily work routine.

THE PROGRAM'S EFFECTS

Analysis via qualitative formative evaluation by program participants revealed three main effects that participants attributed to the program's first year of implementation: an increased awareness of effective practices, an enhanced atmosphere of openness and teacher efficacy, and greater utilization of teachers' knowledge.

INCREASED AWARENESS OF EFFECTIVE PRACTICES

Most teachers were grateful for the opportunity provided by the program to discover staff members' professional tacit knowledge, which had previously gone unrecognized. Participants acknowledged that through this collective learning process, "professional knowledge became public and visible to the eye, exposed," as a communication teacher asserted. Findings revealed that the process of listening to colleagues and uncovering the detailed path that led to their successes illuminated various pedagogical strategies that participants considered to be relevant to their teaching practices.

> I am a veteran teacher; however, listening to others' success stories exposed me to new pedagogical approaches that had never occurred to me before.
>
> —a high school geography coordinator

> Participants were exposed to unconventional successful practices.
>
> —a middle school history teacher

> It revealed other and new sides of teachers' professional work. These other sides came up because this forum provided teachers who generally do not discuss their professional practices with an opportunity to share them.
>
> —a high school information technology teacher

> The learning forum provided the opportunity to hear about practices that cannot be described during hectic daily schoolwork.
>
> —a high school math teacher

> The learning forum helped teachers uncover their hidden professional knowledge and consequently learn from each other.
>
> —a high school principal

Thus, through this collective inquiry, teachers became familiar with their colleagues' successful practices that probably would not have been shared otherwise. Collective learning from successes helped teachers to become knowledgeable about their colleagues' professional expertise, which would not have been accessible to them otherwise.

Some participants gave examples of successful methods learned during the ongoing collective learning process. These methods may be classified as follows:

- *Methods for improving instruction*: "I learned new ways to teach in heterogeneous classrooms."

- *Methods for improving student achievements*: "I learned how to plan my lesson better as a means for improving my students' outcomes."

- *Methods for overcoming discipline problems*: "I learned how to empower students who were classic troublemakers by providing them with various roles and responsibilities during classroom activities."

- *Methods for enhancing student motivation*: "I learned how to help turn a student with a poor self-image into a motivated one."

- *Methods related to school organization*: "Based on the successful experience my colleague described, I understood how to hold the ninth-grade art fair so that it would be a success."

In this regard, listening to colleagues' successes provided teachers with new perspectives for interpreting situations, analyzing their contexts, and providing potential solutions and avenues for actions. Nevertheless, listening to colleagues' success stories led to a reconfirmation of familiar practices as well:

> I learned through listening to successful stories, which had similar characteristics to my practice context. It strengthened my belief in my teaching practices.
>
> —a middle school math teacher

Inquiring into pedagogical successes provided collective assurance of already-known pedagogical frames of mind and action used in classrooms. Thus, on the one hand, inquiring into colleagues' successful practices resulted in exploration and discovery of new teaching strategies, while on the other hand, these forums provided a reconfirmation of time-tested strategies through collective assurance. Interestingly, the interplay between exploration and reconfirmation can also be viewed from the organizational change perspective:

> The inquiry into successes focused our attention on various forces operating in schools as well as pointed out the teachers who push for change versus others who prefer the current situation.
>
> —a middle school art teacher

This may be the case where collective learning from success has exposed both the motivating and the inhibiting forces related to school change.

ENHANCED ATMOSPHERE OF OPENNESS
AND TEACHERS' SENSE OF EFFICACY

Practitioners in the 20 participating schools highlighted the positive learning atmosphere established among staff members as a result of the program, characterizing it as

> a pleasant and supportive atmosphere . . . an atmosphere of mutual appreciation and acceptance.
>
> —a high school biology teacher

> an open and ongoing dialogue among teachers with regard to their stories of success . . . where teachers learned to listen to one another.
>
> —a middle school English teacher

> an atmosphere of interest in learning from one another's experiences, which enhanced feelings of partnership, togetherness, and group pride.
>
> —a high school literature teacher

Thus, this positive atmosphere made teachers feel comfortable in opening up to the rest of the staff:

> The teachers felt a pleasant, non-condescending openness and thus engaged in dialogue without fear. Each teacher listened to the other, and we formulated a uniform language toward the students. Progress was good due to the professional teachers' feeling that they belonged and could recount their successes.
>
> —a middle school literature teacher

One learning coordinator summed up this improved atmosphere of openness as contributing to teachers' sense of efficacy:

> I learned a lot about my abilities as well as those of my students and staff members, too. I know that, to this day, many of the teachers who participated in the process still talk about successes more than they talk about failures.
>
> *(Continued)*

(Continued)

There is a real need to learn from each other about success, to encourage and strengthen each other as a learning community. The process that the teachers undergo as a result of learning from successes changes their way of thinking. . . . For us, it strengthened the teaching staff and created new relationships between people. . . . It contributed a great deal to the staff, and it made the group much more cohesive. You learn how to listen and not only talk. . . . Significant learning took place as there was a lot of dialogue and abundant cooperation and openness on the personal level.

However, it is important to note that not all participants shared this positive orientation. It appeared that, in several schools, the lack of an open atmosphere hindered implementation of the process of collective inquiry into successes, as it could not be effectively applied. In these schools, it even resulted in cynicism and suspicions among colleagues with regard to their ability to learn together as a staff:

Not all participants in the circle of learners felt safe enough to be open with colleagues and to share their success stories.

—a high school literature teacher

Experienced teachers think they know everything, which tends to undermine successes of novice and less experienced teachers.

—a high school homeroom teacher

However, overall, the collective learning generated from focusing on past successes fostered a shared belief in the capacity of schools and their staff members to succeed in their tasks and to learn from their experiences:

We started talking about successes, not only about failures. . . . The atmosphere was more pleasant, more relaxed. As soon as everyone gets involved and takes the idea seriously, and we don't just let it fade away but are consistent, we see that we can learn together from successes. . . . This gave us a different view, a new perspective, which helped a lot with the way we later faced our students.

—a high school learning coordinator

> There was openness on the part of the teachers, there was cooperation, and the fact was that there were teachers who did succeed. Through them, we realized that we, too, could succeed and that we could learn together.
>
> —a high school math teacher

Thus, learning from success reinforced participants' learning competency and instilled in them a sense of appreciation, respect, and even wonder at the value of their own and their students' accomplishments:

> The fact that your success was announced in front of a group of teachers and collectively analyzed is like a self-fulfilling prophecy that arouses feelings of pride. It is an essential process in building a professional team, because as we all know, teachers rarely receive positive feedback.
>
> —a middle school communications teacher

This success-based orientation in a supportive atmosphere enhanced participants' sense of efficacy regarding their own expertise as well as that of their colleagues:

> Teachers who told their success stories called me on the phone to say how much this process had helped them and gave them a chance to talk about what they were doing, and how they felt satisfaction and self-confidence thanks to the revelation of their abilities.
>
> —a high school science teacher

Nevertheless, several teachers indicated that they rarely, if ever, experienced successes in their professional work:

> I was sitting with colleagues who immediately spoke of professional successes. I wondered why it was so hard for me to find a single success story in my entire work experience.
>
> —a high school English teacher

Two learning coordinators also acknowledged that the learning workshops frustrated those teachers who perceived themselves as unsuccessful. Hence, the data suggested that on the one hand, the collective learning process enhanced successful teachers' sense of efficacy whereas on the other hand, this success-based orientation could also raise doubts as to certain teachers' professional expertise.

Collective learning from success served as an organizational database that collected information from individual teachers into a common, shared body of knowledge. This joint accumulation of knowledge about the school's successes was recognized by the program's qualitative evaluators as an important program outcome, described as

> taking stock of the school's arsenal of pedagogical tools for the benefit of all teachers.
>
> —a high school science teacher

> a learning process that enabled us to understand what our resources for future activities would be.
>
> —a middle school history teacher

> facilitating better use of the knowledge embedded within us, something we seldom do and know how to do, thereby contributing to our collective knowledge.
>
> —a high school history teacher

The learning-from-success process, then, encoded individual pedagogical practices into shared knowledge that was distinct from the individual knowledge and surpassed it:

> We were asked to tell of an achievement related to the children in class and I saw teachers' enthusiasm. Teachers took tips from each other, and even if they took just one tip, it was worth it. . . . I saw many teachers' excitement, both those who recounted their experiences and those who listened and learned from them.
>
> —a high school literature teacher

From a systemic point of view, analyzing successes in various subject areas led teachers to acknowledge the interrelations among them. Teachers stressed that the forum of learning from success

> facilitated an exchange of ideas, approaches, and professional knowledge between teachers of different subjects who had no opportunity to learn together in the past.
>
> —a high school homeroom teacher

> enriched teachers' interdisciplinary learning and enabled them to transfer knowledge and teaching strategies from one content area to another.
>
> —a middle school art teacher

> helped teachers to extract the knowledge about successful experiences that resides within each subject area for the benefit of other subject areas.
>
> —a high school geography teacher

A science teacher aptly summed up how the program's collective exchange of ideas exploring colleagues' successes in school led to significantly greater utilization of teachers' own knowledge that had previously been inaccessible while also exposing the underlying pedagogical interrelationships among various disciplines and subjects:

> The program contributed to the development of the personal self as well as the professional self and to the methods of instruction. . . . Those who reaped the benefits were the students. As a result of learning from success, every time I had some successful event or occurrence, I brought the staff in so that they could learn from it and implement it in their classes. . . . It has already become a part of us. . . . At first, teachers had an ocean of knowledge, but it remained closed off, inside them; now the material is out in the open and [is] all very well-organized. In addition to the workshops where each teacher shared his or her experiences, there is a special folder with all the success stories, which anyone can access. This sharing opened up many possibilities because each person was exposed to the broad picture of how the school system functions, which created a sense of pride in the school. At first, each of us was alone, "inside his or her own castle" so to speak, but then, suddenly, we were exposed to the successes of the entire school and could see that there was a reward for all our labor. The cooperation tended to remain within each grade-level, as different grade-levels have differing needs. But new ideas came up and we upgraded our entire outlook. Cooperation with the extended staff members for all classes has blossomed. Each team has a teacher who is responsible for bringing in the materials for the collective learning as well as documenting the analyzed successes.

Furthermore, in several schools, attempts were made to disseminate the principles gleaned from the inquiry into successful practices for the use of various forums (e.g., subject coordinators). Whereas seven of the 20 schools acknowledged a successful dissemination of success principles to other forums (such as to teachers who had not participated in the circle of learners), other schools encountered quite different responses. For example, a history teacher stated that "a request to consider this successful model in other circles at the school was immediately rejected." Thus, we can see that attempts to spread the successful practices to other learning forums were welcomed by some while totally rejected by others.

CASE ILLUSTRATIONS: THE NATIONAL PROGRAM AS APPLIED IN THREE SCHOOLS

To see what may be learned from the learning-from-success program, documentation that three different schools posted on the learning-from-success website was analyzed. These schools were selected in an attempt to represent different geographic regions and different types of student populations. School A is a Jewish high school from a rural area (400 students, 30 teachers). School B is a Muslim middle school from a rural area (500 students, 43 teachers). School C is a Jewish high school from an urban area (700 students, 60 teachers).

To enrich understanding of possible routes that may be taken along the learning-from-success journey, this chapter next presents three cases of schools' program implementation while analyzing (a) the milestones all along the process (Table 5.2); (b) the organizational frameworks that the three developmental teams utilized to implement the program (Table 5.3); (c) a detailed example of one success per school that their collective learning groups analyzed and documented (Table 5.4); (d) an example of the circle of learners' feedback in each school regarding the program's "learning about learning" component, when group participants reflected jointly on how they had learned and communicated together during the collective inquiry into successful practices (Table 5.5); and (e) program outcomes (Table 5.6). Importantly, the three schools' learning-from-success processes were site- and topic-specific. The detailed information presented next on these three schools elucidates the variability and flexibility of the learning-from-success model, which offers structured guidelines but not a rigid "cookbook" approach. This fluidity should encourage school and district leaders to move forward to implement learning from success because each school may adapt the success-based learning model to its own needs, goals, leadership style, and limitations.

MILESTONES IN THE PROGRAM'S IMPLEMENTATION

The analyzed school documentation texts furnish a road map authored by the circle of learner's participants themselves, which facilitates understanding of the program's dynamics by means of forums' descriptions of milestones all along the process (Ellenbogen-Frankovits et al., 2011). Table 5.2 describes the milestones in the learning process that each of the three schools identified. Each school's activity is described in a separate column. The numbers in each column are used to distinguish between various milestones in the process. These milestones are based on the three schools' documentation of their developmental team's meetings as well as the summarizing interviews conducted with the members of the developmental teams at the conclusion of the program's first year.

TABLE 5.2 Milestones in Implementing the Learning-From-Success Program as Documented by Each of the Three Schools

SCHOOL A (RURAL HIGH SCHOOL)	SCHOOL B (RURAL MIDDLE SCHOOL)	SCHOOL C (URBAN HIGH SCHOOL)
1. After the principal's suggestion to discuss the program meets with fierce opposition, she consults the developmental team.	1. The principal decides to implement the program with all the teachers in the school. He sees it as being within the scope of his authority to make such decisions.	1. The superintendent begins by saying that she has come to give her blessing to the program. She adds that she will not be able to participate regularly in the forum's meetings, but she will receive updates on the contents.
2. The learning coordinator speaks with each teacher personally about the program and hears responses. She represents the homeroom teachers' voices in the developmental team.	2. The principal assigns a special time to the program outside of other routine school activities. This specific time, to be dedicated to meetings about learning from successes, requires all teachers in the school to participate while the principal explains the importance of the issue.	2. The learning coordinator raises questions as to the nature of her own role. She sees it mainly as that of a documenter. This leads to a discussion about the central role of the learning coordinator in establishing a learning group, setting a fixed time for learning, formulating learning issues, leading, and ensuring ongoing documentation.
3. Teachers request an outside consultant with whom they can discuss their feelings of not belonging to the staff and feelings of distrust before they begin the program.	3. The principal summons the teachers for three sessions to get acquainted with the program, during which he presents it through lectures.	3. The principal decides to present the program to the teachers during a preparation workshop for the new school year.
4. The principal and the learning coordinator consult with the superintendent and learning accompanist in the developmental team and ask for the learning coordinator's help in presenting the program to the teachers.	4. After the program has been presented to them, the teachers continue to meet during the set time for the program and decide to begin the process of learning from personal successes.	4. The members of the forum immediately join the mission, and each contributes his or her ideas. The principal and the learning coordinator decide on the specific success story from which they wish to learn, and they ask one of the teachers to present her success to the staff.
5. Teachers agree to hear about the program but claim that they have no collective successes and that personal successes are private and do not concern everyone.	5. Successful use of the built-in method for learning from success pleases participants and they sense satisfaction to the point of agreeing to continue the process.	5. The principal presents the program to all the teachers by creating a suitable atmosphere, discussing the program, and providing initial training for three and a half hours.
6. The learning coordinator prepares invitations to the circle of learners, recruits the teachers, talks with them, and persuades them to participate.	6. Learning from success takes place in the school's various professional teams.	6. The program is delivered by the learning coordinator as part of a teacher training course for teachers who are interested in it.
7. The developmental team accepts the learning accompanist's idea—that teachers begin a learning-from-success program while also discussing school difficulties.	7. The principal speaks about the school's success in reducing violence in school in recent years. The learning companion marvels at the story and helps participants learn from this success.	

(Continued)

TABLE 5.2 (Continued)

SCHOOL A (RURAL HIGH SCHOOL)	SCHOOL B (RURAL MIDDLE SCHOOL)	SCHOOL C (URBAN HIGH SCHOOL)
8. The learning coordinator opens the learning-from-success workshop with a lecture in which she presents the program and imparts its research tools to both teachers and students.	8. The principal and teachers combine retrospective learning from success with the planning of new actions aimed at addressing current school issues. This inspires wonder, and participants feel that they have gained new insight into their school's activities.	7. There is considerable emphasis on practicing the method of learning from success, but the teachers are quite embarrassed by the need to share their successes and sense discomfort.
9. Teachers accept the proposal and choose the school's new art track as a success story, as its participants are students with slim chances of success on the matriculation exams. A decision is reached to invite the art teacher and her students to the school's circle of learners for the purpose of learning from success.	9. Teachers disseminate learning from success to informal learning spaces, such as the school kitchen, the yard, and meetings with parents.	8. The teachers practice using the method while enjoying increasing confidence.
10. The art teacher and her students join the circle of learners, and the inquiry format for learning from the art track's success is applied in two sessions, creating a very surprising experience—a turning point—for all participating teachers and students.	10. Learning from success echoes in many ways in various domains of school life.	9. Some teachers note that they are surprised by their habit of ignoring or minimizing their successes, and they notice how it affects their tendency to focus on problems and on the "dark side" of their occupation.
11. At the third meeting, the teachers meet without the students, and express their surprise regarding the process of learning from success together with their students. They begin discussing the structural tension between the reality of their school and the desired state of their school.	11. Parents are invited to participate in learning from success.	10. Teachers find many successes at school and feel that they are becoming accustomed to learning from success.
12. The teachers create different forums for learning from success, thus influencing the school's organizational structure. The program is also used to directly address issues relating to the school's organizational context.		11. The teachers spend the entire first year studying successes. They connect with other schools and learn from their experience as well.
13. Parents are invited to participate in the circle of learners.		

ORGANIZATIONAL FRAMEWORKS UTILIZED BY THE THREE DEVELOPMENTAL TEAMS TO IMPLEMENT THE PROGRAM

As seen in Table 5.2, each of these three schools traveled a different path on their journey toward learning from success, but all three eventually reached a point where they succeeded in meeting the program's two goals of inculcating ongoing learning from success and leveraging that learning process to achieve desired school outcomes. Following this comparison of the three schools' milestones over the first year of the learning-from-success program's implementation, conclusions could be drawn regarding the organizational framework that each school utilized in order to implement the program. Table 5.3 presents this analysis of the three developmental teams' decision-making and organizational structures (Ellenbogen-Frankovits et al., 2011).

DETAILED EXAMPLE OF ONE SUCCESS PER SCHOOL, ANALYZED AND DOCUMENTED BY THEIR COLLECTIVE LEARNING GROUPS

Each school chose to learn from the successes that took place within its walls. Yet, examples of different schools' success stories can help situate learning about the program's applicability and usefulness. In Table 5.4, each school's first success is presented, as taken from each school's online documentation of its learning process. To be recalled, learning from success takes place through the use of a built-in structured method not only for learning but also for systematic documentation to maximize transfer of learned knowledge to new situations and practitioners. With regard to their process of learning from successes, participants in the program used a standardized format for documenting success, where the numbers in each column distinguish the different components of each stage for exploring that school's success story. For example, in the stage of "objective evidence of success," School A documented five testimonies, School B documented only one, and School C documented four.

EACH SCHOOL'S FEEDBACK ON LEARNING ABOUT LEARNING FROM SUCCESS IN THE CIRCLE OF LEARNERS

As described earlier in this chapter, in line with the national program's two-component structure, the core of each collective learning session was devoted to analyzing success stories and, toward the end of each session, participants were encouraged to reflect jointly on how they had learned and communicated together that day during their collective inquiry into successful practices. According to the documentation, schools' circles of learners often concluded with the question, *How did we learn today?* Table 5.5 presents some examples of participants' answers as documented by the three schools.

TABLE 5.3   The Organizational Framework for Implementing the Learning-From-Success Program in the Three Schools

ORGANIZATIONAL DECISION	SCHOOL A (RURAL HIGH SCHOOL)	SCHOOL B (RURAL MIDDLE SCHOOL)	SCHOOL C (URBAN HIGH SCHOOL)
Way of presenting the program	The principal and learning coordinator give a single presentation to all teachers. The learning coordinator attempts to persuade teachers to participate in the program by providing explanations via personal conversations and a written invitation.	The principal summons the teachers for three sessions of acquaintance with the program. He dedicates these three meetings to presenting the program through lectures to all the teachers in the school.	The principal plans the presentation of the program's implementation plan in detail. He then presents the program for 3.5 hours to all teachers. The presentation includes how to create a suitable atmosphere, formal information, and practice of the method.
Mentoring the program	The program is mentored by the principal and the learning coordinator.	The learning coordinator mentors the program.	The learning coordinator mentors the program.
Specifying place and time	The circle of learners is open to all teachers and held every two weeks during teachers' regular meetings.	The principal assigns a new, permanent setting for the program at the school with the participation of all teachers every two weeks.	The circle of learners is held every two weeks under the guidance of the principal and learning coordinator as part of a teacher training course.
Participation conditions	Participation in the school's circle of learners is part of a teachers' meeting, but participation is voluntary. Most of the teachers choose to participate.	Participation in the school's circle of learners is obligatory for all teachers. Those who do not wish to participate receive an explanation about the circle of learners' importance.	Participation in the first meeting is mandatory. The program is presented to all high school teachers, but later, the participation is voluntary as part of teacher training, and teachers are free to choose whether to participate or not.

ORGANIZATIONAL DECISION	SCHOOL A (RURAL HIGH SCHOOL)	SCHOOL B (RURAL MIDDLE SCHOOL)	SCHOOL C (URBAN HIGH SCHOOL)
Initial organization of school's circle of learners	A short-term circle of learners (two meetings) for teachers and students is organized. Participants learn from the success story of the art track according to the seven-stage inquiry format. Subsequently, they begin a long-term circle of learners aimed at clarifying the difficulties of teachers at the school. The teachers are asked to describe the current situation and the desired one.	A two-year circle of learners is planned. The teachers are asked to recall success stories, and one of the teachers tells her personal success story about her transition from being a problematic student to becoming a schoolteacher. The discussion of her personal success story excites the other teachers, and they decide that in each session, they will discuss another personal success story according to the seven-stage inquiry format.	A one-year circle of learners is organized by the principal and the learning coordinator. The latter asks teachers to explain why they chose to participate in the circle of learners. The group conducts a discussion about successes and tacit knowledge at the school and then sets the rules for participating in the circle of learners: keeping timetables, listening to each other, and maintaining discretion.
Composition and scope of participants in the program	The first circle of learners is attended by 20 teachers, six students, and four members of the developmental team. The second circle of learners is attended by 20 teachers (educators, professional teachers, and management staff).	The circle of learners is attended by the entire school staff of 46 teachers. Later on, students are invited to the circle of learners as well.	The first meeting is attended by all 60 teachers; the second meeting is attended by 22 teachers who choose to participate. A group of 13 participants—members of the management team and some of the teachers—is formed as the steady forum for learning from success (comprising 20% of all teachers who chose to participate).
Fitting the program into the curriculum	At the end of the first year, the program is integrated into the system as part of the ongoing work at the school.	The program has been integrated into the system of teachers since its inception.	The program is not integrated into the system but rather is held as part of a teacher training course only.

TABLE 5.4 Collective Learning Group's Analysis of Past Success as Documented by the Three Schools

	INQUIRY STAGE	SCHOOL A (RURAL HIGH SCHOOL) SUCCESS OF THE ART TRACK	SCHOOL B (RURAL MIDDLE SCHOOL) SUCCESS IN MITIGATING VIOLENCE	SCHOOL C (URBAN HIGH SCHOOL) SUCCESS IN FORGING A MATH TEACHER TEAM
1	Success description	Six struggling students joined a new art track for an experimental project and eventually passed matriculation exams with excellent grades.	The principal's intervention in addition to the recruitment of teachers as well as the parents' committee led to a decrease in violence in the school.	A teacher who had come from another school succeeded in forming a team of math teachers.
2	Before	1. Students had not studied art for matriculation exams. 2. There was no alternative framework for struggling students.	1. There were many reports by teachers and students about incidents of violence: harassment, assaults, cursing, and threats. 2. The centers of violence were in the restrooms, on the way home, in the schoolyard, and in classrooms during recess.	1. The school had high high rates of turnover—new math teachers coming and leaving. 2. Individual teachers worked without cooperation.
3	After	1. An art track was established, leading to matriculation exams. 2. The struggling students achieved good grades on the matriculation exams.	1. There was a sharp drop in reports of violence. 2. Teachers complained less about cases of violence. 3. Parents said that the learning atmosphere was very good and that they did not encounter violence. 4. An open and ongoing dialogue was carried out in the school about violence.	1. The team was cohesive, welcoming, open, and accepting.
4	Objective proof of success	1. Before, there was no such track with matriculation exams, and afterwards, there was one. 2. Every student who started the program completed it and passed the matriculation exam.	1. A decrease occurred in the number of violent incidents from 200 to 180 in the first year to 150 in the second year.	1. Stable math team was formed. 2. All staff came to the training courses and became a learning team. 3. The math team became socially cohesive and was allocated a special table in the teachers' room for only the mathematics staff.

102

INQUIRY STAGE	SCHOOL A (RURAL HIGH SCHOOL) SUCCESS OF THE ART TRACK	SCHOOL B (RURAL MIDDLE SCHOOL) SUCCESS IN MITIGATING VIOLENCE	SCHOOL C (URBAN HIGH SCHOOL) SUCCESS IN FORGING A MATH TEACHER TEAM
	3. Students who studied in the program recommended it to younger students. 4. The grades on the matriculation exams were high. 5. Some students continued the track by expanding their art program study units.		4. Team collaboration blossomed. 5. The team was ready to help with various school projects.
5 Unexpected side effects	1. Students in the program gained self-confidence and chose to study additional units in the art program for matriculation exams. 2. One of the students who had neglected her language studies was encouraged by her success in art and finally studied for her language matriculation exam the following year. 3. Students understood that it was worth investing in order to succeed. 4. Success motivated students: "Since first grade, I've been hearing that I have potential and nothing much has happened with it. Here, I have finally experienced success!"	1. Students became happy to be affiliated with the school. 2. Students were willing to participate in most of the school's activities. 3. Students stayed at school in the afternoon for various classes. 4. Students showed a willingness to participate in fundraising campaigns in the surrounding village. 5. The school was admired and praised by many of the village residents.	1. Personal contacts were established between team members (celebrating birthdays, holding joint meals, mutual help in personal matters, etc.). 2. Success rates in mathematics matriculation exams rose. 3. There was a rise in the percentage of students studying more advanced levels of mathematics.
6 Activities/ actions	1. The art teacher got the management and the teaching staff to help her find teaching tools and create an appropriate learning environment. 2. The teacher came in during the afternoon (at the expense of her own free time).	1. The principal mobilized the entire team to combat violence. 2. Violent students got an opportunity to succeed as stewards at school fairs. 3. Respectful and special attitudes were expressed toward students.	1. The teachers listened to others' ideas. 2. Teachers consulted with team members. 3. Teachers made use of others' knowledge and experience. 4. The teachers formed programs, lists, books, tests, and worksheets together.

(Continued)

TABLE 5.4 (Continued)

INQUIRY STAGE	SCHOOL A (RURAL HIGH SCHOOL) SUCCESS OF THE ART TRACK	SCHOOL B (RURAL MIDDLE SCHOOL) SUCCESS IN MITIGATING VIOLENCE	SCHOOL C (URBAN HIGH SCHOOL) SUCCESS IN FORGING A MATH TEACHER TEAM
	3. The teacher enabled students who failed the theoretical test to succeed on a practical one. 4. The teacher accompanied her demands from the students with explanations of their rationale. 5. The teacher gave personal attention to each student while considering his or her needs. 6. The teacher used the feedback she received from her students to correct and adjust her lessons accordingly.	4. Students felt proud of their performance. 5. Students from "warring factions" were brought into joint sports activities at school. 6. Personal conversations were held with students in informal spaces (yard, kitchen, at home). 7. Students were invited to teachers' meetings to hear what helped and what bothered students.	5. Teachers created a new position of teacher/mentor for new teachers. 6. Math teachers were constantly going for refresher courses. 7. The teachers delegated authority, sharing various tasks with others. 8. The teachers visited new teachers' classes. 9. The teachers provided tips and guidance. 10. The math teachers sometimes met in the afternoon, after the school day.
7 Principles of action	1. Cooperation between school officials 2. Openness in the relationship between teacher and students 3. Personal contact with and attention to students according to their personal needs 4. Willingness to explain requirements' significance to students and adapt tasks to their abilities 5. Balance between flexibility, openness, and understanding of students on the one hand and setting clear boundaries on the other 6. Creating an atmosphere that enabled true mutual contact between teacher and students, with each side urging the other to invest more and improve	1. Integration of violent students into school events while respecting them and giving them significant roles in the school 2. Giving personal attention to students 3. Showing respect for students to improve their self-perception, motivation to learn, and cooperation 4. Creation of a family-like atmosphere in the school 5. Bringing students in to participate in teacher meetings and listening to them express their needs 6. Recruitment of the entire team of teachers and bringing them together for the purpose of fulfilling the mission	1. Preparation for joint learning; regular and continuous meetings designed to stimulate team members to cooperate in preparing tasks and to exercise reflective thinking 2. Generosity by veteran teachers spending time mentoring young teachers 3. Joint work to replace former professional isolation 4. Redesign of the role of professional coordinator as a professional facilitator and team developer 5. Development of personal contacts between members of the teaching staff

TABLE 5.5   How Did We Learn Today?

SCHOOL A (RURAL HIGH SCHOOL)	SCHOOL B (RURAL MIDDLE SCHOOL)	SCHOOL C (URBAN HIGH SCHOOL)
⋏ "I learned how she succeeded, but I do not know if I can succeed. My envy of her success weakens me; it does not help me learn."	⋏ "I learned from going forward and backward again. It's a positive pendulum, back and forth, but I do make progress."	⋏ "I learned from listening."
⋏ "I learned from listening and comparing."	⋏ "I learned from the encounter with people with different perspectives."	⋏ "I checked what was said and applied it to work in my team."
⋏ "Our sitting in a circle (and not in rows like last time) created an open and friendly atmosphere."	⋏ "I learned from external feedback. I have my own self-criticism and criticism from others, which is more objective and sometimes even more optimistic."	⋏ "I learned from comparison, but it made me frustrated. I do not know how to do it. It doesn't happen on my team, so where did I go wrong? And how can I learn from what I've heard here?"
	⋏ "The documentation helped me focus; without documentation I get lost."	⋏ "I learned from participation, something nonverbal that says a lot in body language. I learned from nonverbal connecting."

PROGRAM OUTCOMES: CHANGES IN
THE SCHOOL FOLLOWING THE PROGRAM

In the summarizing interviews with members of the developmental team, four types of outcomes were identified that may be attributed to the impact of the learning-from-success program:

- Broad use of the learning-from-success method

- Creation of new learning frameworks following the program

- Changes in norms, atmosphere, and relationships at school

- Changes in relationships between teachers and students

Table 5.6 presents the results described in the summarizing interviews with members of each school's developmental team.

Overall, all three of these schools implemented the same national program, but each school initiated and operated it in a unique way that suited its leadership style and particular context. Each school used the program's built-in forums and methods to systematically organize its activities while maintaining its own freedom of choice in terms of contents and specific activities.

FURTHER EXPLORATIONS

Implementation of this national program for learning from success in 20 schools raised several issues for further deliberation. First, the program's evaluation efforts pinpointed a major question deserving further scrutiny: the extent to which knowledge gained via this program was being disseminated between schools. Knowledge explored in the circle of learners' forums was posted on the Ministry of Education's Internet site. While these materials could easily be accessed and were judged by their stakeholders as generalizable and actionable for applications outside the specific school that created them, there was little evidence that these learning-from-success products were indeed being viewed by other schools, including those schools participating in this program. At that point, despite the program's impact on within-school communication processes, it appeared that less had been accomplished in terms of between-school knowledge diffusion. Future documentation and dissemination efforts need to seek out ways to make the collectively explored knowledge more accessible so that it can be reflected upon by other learning communities.

A second issue was that although teachers who had participated in the circle of learners clearly indicated that they had learned considerably from one another, the program's evaluation did not offer data on how this collective learning process might have affected real-time classroom practices. Can learning from success

THE COLLECTIVE WISDOM OF PRACTICE

TABLE 5.6 National Program's Outcomes as Documented by the Three Schools

OUTCOME	SCHOOL A (RURAL HIGH SCHOOL)	SCHOOL B (RURAL MIDDLE SCHOOL)	SCHOOL C (URBAN HIGH SCHOOL)
1. Broadened use of the learning-from-success method	Teachers from the circle of learners began starting their routine school meetings (not explicit learning-from-success meetings) by identifying success in classes. When teachers in these meetings raised issues pertaining to difficult students, peers from the circle of learners began asking them to think about successes they have had with students and to suggest ideas as to what could be done to succeed in new challenging situations as well.	Teachers from various professional teams learned how to question each other to effectively learn from one another's success. Teachers also began using learning from success in class. For example, if a student succeeded in completing a task in the classroom, the teacher pointed it out to the class and questioned the student as to what he or she did to succeed and then talked about it in class.	The teachers reflected on learning from success with a group of colleagues, referring to it as a journey and choosing partners for the journey. They weighed successes' benefits versus costs, documenting their courses of action and learning and leaving room for unresolved issues.
2. Creating new learning frameworks following the program	As a result of the program, new frameworks were created in the school. The leading team encouraged teachers to visit other teachers' classes to learn from each other. The developmental team decided to institutionalize this learning method, and each teacher was assigned hours of visits to other teachers' classes for learning purposes.	A regular forum for learning from school successes was established, attended by all teachers in the school and taking place at a fixed time as part of the weekly schedule. Teacher and student forums for learning from success were established.	Following the program, the school established a learning center for students with learning disabilities based on the learning-from-success ideas.

(Continued)

TABLE 5.6 (Continued)

OUTCOME	SCHOOL A (RURAL HIGH SCHOOL)	SCHOOL B (RURAL MIDDLE SCHOOL)	SCHOOL C (URBAN HIGH SCHOOL)
3. Changes in norms, atmosphere, and relationships at school (excerpts from developmental team members' summarizing interviews)	≻ "There is an atmosphere of openness among teachers. People get respect and others listen. No one rules out someone else's ideas or thoughts." ≻ "The feeling is that everyone became much more responsible and conscientious. Many teachers are to be given credit for the program's success." ≻ "Teachers are enjoying the new school practice." ≻ "Teachers are willing to share and learn from their successes. The atmosphere has changed: Instead of an atmosphere of self-defensiveness and refusal to reveal private successes to others, there is an atmosphere of willingness to be exposed, communicate, and learn."	≻ "Teachers talk more about success." ≻ "Teachers are more receptive to criticism from each other, but the big change is teachers' greater willingness to accept criticism from students, which used to be perceived as a violation of the teachers' authority. The program led to a change on the moral and normative levels. This change was difficult for most teachers and for the principal as well, but they were aware of the need to make it."	≻ "The program created more openness and readiness to talk about successes and failures at school." ≻ "Teachers cooperate and allow themselves to share successes, encourage each other, and, (at times) also to criticize." ≻ "The program created an atmosphere of enthusiasm, which goes along with the activity in this realm."
4. Changes in relationships between teachers and students	After learning-from-success sessions, many teachers expressed their positive feelings about the change that had transpired in their relationships with their students. They began viewing them with different eyes and liked this encounter. From this point on, it was clear to them that partnership with students in learning from success was essential.	Teachers showed more interest, openness, and flexibility and listened more to students' ideas. The learning coordinator reported that the teachers had learned that personal attention raises student achievement levels.	The school psychologist reported that she felt an improvement in the school atmosphere—more conversations, contacts, and dialogue between teachers and students.

actually penetrate classroom walls? Can collective learning from successful practices serve as a genuine resource for teachers' innovative practices in the classroom? Put differently, can learning from success serve as a link between school restructuring efforts and innovations at the classroom level? What are the connections between systemic processes of learning from success and student outcomes?

Possible answers to these questions may be related to the principles of action that circles of learners drew from the abstraction or generalization of participants' success-promoting actions, which had been exposed through the group's post-action reviews while questioning the success stories' protagonists. The goal of identifying *principles of action* as a central part of the collective learning group's interview format should always be to reach common insights as to the actions that contributed to a certain success so that they can be repeated in different settings and contexts. The key to creating appropriate, generalizable principles of action is to formulate them in such a way that, on the one hand, they are anchored in the specific success-promoting actions and, on the other hand, they are applicable to varied and broad contexts. This duality of specificity and commonality will enable principles of action to be put to beneficial use and help obtain desired results under diverse circumstances. As discussed in Chapter 4, spurred by this formative evaluation process from the national program initiative, a fuller multistep inquiry format was developed. This more comprehensive multistep inquiry format provides practical guidelines for converting actions to action principles as part of efforts to help learning-from-success participants make the transition from micro to macro perspectives.

In sum, this chapter discussed the national program of Learning from Success as Leverage for Schoolwide Learning, exploring both processes and outcomes of this program within participating schools. Nevertheless, does collective learning from success provide staff members with the necessary capacity to inquire into pressing school issues? The next chapter delves into an important question facing educators: Can we switch gears, thus envisioning learning from successes and learning from failures/problems as complementing and nourishing one another in enacting educators' professional wisdoms of practice?

CHAPTER 6

Switching Gears

Learning From Success and Learning From Problems as a Catalyst to Growth and Change

> The national evaluation of elementary schools includes a school climate assessment. Our school's results are very high in this area. But I know our school, and I don't think the situation is really that satisfactory. However, for me, the integration of learning from both successes and problems that we've learned here has shown me that we probably do several things well after all, and we have to shed light on them collaboratively. We mustn't only seek improvement by learning how we overcame our problems; we also must be able to integrate learning from our right moves.
>
> —an elementary school principal

As elaborated in Chapter 2, learning from problems has been lauded as beneficial for organizational learning in schools because it stimulates a high willingness to consider alternatives, critiques traditional working patterns, and generates an unfreezing process in which organization members are able to perceive the need for change, while learning from success has been acclaimed for its potential to enhance reflection on effective practices, create positive organizational memory, and generate a commitment to and an investment in learning among diverse members of a school community. Yet, each of these two collective learning approaches' pitfalls and risks have also been delineated in prior chapters. Now, considering that both learning from success and learning from problems offer advantages and disadvantages, strengths and weaknesses, the current chapter explores the usefulness of schools' dual-pronged inquiry into both successful and problematic aspects of professional practices (Madsen & Desai, 2010). In particular, this chapter discusses how learning from success and learning from problems can actually complement and nourish one another.

Traditionally, schools are accustomed to focusing on past failures and problems as well-accepted means for constructing their future. In this way, learning in schools to date has been highly predisposed to a process of detecting and correcting errors. This problem-oriented form of inquiry has conditioned learning efforts exclusively toward things that have gone wrong. In this regard, Cook and Yanow (1996) argued that contemplating only what went wrong is not necessarily relevant, or sufficient, for organizational life. Thus, schools may benefit from studying both successful and problematic/failed events because "success fosters reliability, whereas failure fosters resilience" (Sitkin, 1996, p. 551). We can no longer depend solely on either learning from success or learning from problems as a source of positive change and growth.

Although both learning from success and learning from problems may be viewed as productive resources for collective learning, practitioners may best benefit from their combination by first initiating learning processes that focus on successes as a stepping-stone toward developing their capacity to deliberate productively on failures and problems. This may seem paradoxical, but it can be explained by envisioning learning from success and learning from problems as a continuum, where learning from success is located at one end, followed by learning from small minor problems, while learning from large-scale and even acute problems or failures is located at the far opposite end of the continuum. When groups begin their collective retrospective learning process with a focus on group members' problems/failures, it may stunt the positive, open atmosphere that is desirable for any effective learning to take place. In other words, engaging in learning from failure without prior experience in learning from success could be likened to asking a first-grade pupil to write the entire alphabet at the end of the first week of school (Schechter, 2001). Without prior positive experiences in learning from successes, the process of learning from failure may be doomed to fail. Specifically, initiating an early process of learning from group members' successes may help them construct the building blocks of teachers' self-confidence (for example, in their skills for respectful peer-questioning and action-oriented discourse about professional practices) without an atmosphere of guilt, blame-throwing, or scapegoating.

Therefore, it seems that starting out by priming group participants to think about successes might be a better choice for initiating the collective learning processes, which can become a self-fulfilling prophecy. In this way, learning from success can serve as a springboard for future productive learning processes in general, including learning from the more stressful and blame-accompanied organizational problems/failures.

That is not to say that learning from problems is not important or necessary. Indeed, the need for a combination of the two learning methods can be illuminated by the aforementioned distinction between single- and double-loop learning. *Single-loop learning*—an instrumental type of learning that leaves the organization's existing values and norms unchanged—is generally produced by learning from success. Such learning can serve as a springboard for *double-loop learning*—learning that generates change in fundamental values and norms—which is generally produced by learning from problems/failures. Learning from daily and sometimes unnoticed successes can provide the resources and experience necessary for future productive learning from failed events. Put differently, productive learning from past experiences should be based on and nurtured by gradually evolving learning from past successful experiences (Schechter, 2011).

Although we recognize the necessity to reach a certain level of learning from failure, we tend to forget that "failure was born of success" (Nonaka, 1985, p. 13), and therefore conscious reflection on successful events is essential in order to establish any sort of productive learning in school communities. In addition, Virany and colleagues (1996) argued that high-performing organizations are "distinct in that they initiate second-order learning not in response to performance decline, but either in anticipation of environmental change or as a response to elevated performance" (p. 325). In this regard, it is argued that while moderately performing schools tend to learn in response to real performance crises (failures), high-level performing schools are proactive; that is, they also learn from successful events as a means of adapting to possible environmental change and/or in order to assess their current situation.

Empirical Illustrations

Switching cognitive gears between learning from problems and learning from success may serve as an optimal analytical framework in today's fast-changing educational scene. To comprehensively assess the value of integrating learning from successes and learning from problems into professional development programs, several research studies have been conducted. The empirical outcomes from such research are presented next, first on incorporating these two learning approaches within teachers' professional education and then on blending these approaches within principals' preparation programs.

TEACHER EDUCATION

Our first study examined preservice teachers during the practicum phase of field teaching as part of their university-based teacher preparation programs (Schechter & Michalsky, 2014). In this research, we explored the value of systematic learning from success as a complementary reflective framework to learning from problems. The study was designed to explore whether prospective science teachers could capitalize on learning from success as a means of stimulating their professional growth by integrating learning from success and learning from problems as reflective frameworks. In this study, both learning-from-success and learning-from-problem reflective frameworks were conceptualized as collective retrospective learning processes in the context of science teaching.

We assessed prospective physics teachers' development along two professional dimensions: (a) *pedagogical content knowledge*, defined as content comprehension, lesson design ability, and actual teaching skills and (b) *sense of self-efficacy*, defined as both personal efficacy in teaching science and science-teaching outcome expectancy. We developed four distinct reflective methods (detailed below) to examine the effect of integrating systematic learning from problematic as well as successful experiences in preparatory programs dealing with pedagogical content knowledge and a sense of teaching efficacy in the realm of physics. Participants were 124 second-year preservice physics teachers at four major research universities. One-way within-subject analyses of variance (ANOVA) with repeated measures were conducted, with posttest performance as the dependent variable and treatment (four reflective groups) as the independent variable.

During the second semester of the practical teaching course, preservice teachers in each of the four groups engaged in reflective analysis immediately after they had completed teaching each lesson to secondary school students (12 lessons in total). Each 40-minute reflective analysis session was conducted under the guidance of a mentor who met with these preservice teachers in the high schools where they delivered their practicum teaching lessons. To analyze successes/problems that had arisen in their lessons, the preservice teachers utilized a five-step reflection format presented linearly, although the steps were interrelated and interdependent. Table 6.1 presents the template that participants used to guide their five steps for collective reflection. As described next, preservice teachers were divided into four groups, all of whom used learning from problems for their reflective analysis, and half of whom additionally used learning from successes. Another goal of the study was to determine whether self-reflection on teaching problems/successes would be more efficient when preservice teachers performed the analytic steps alone (with only the help of the mentor) versus when they performed the steps together with peers in a collective learning forum under the mentor's guidance.

The four groups' reflective methods differed as follows:

P+S+Peers group (n = 31). Each preservice teacher in this group deliberated on a problematic event and then went on to deliberate on a successful event from the lesson he or she had just taught, together with the mentor and three preservice colleagues who had observed the lesson. Using the first question in the five-step reflection format, the preservice teacher reflected first; second to reflect were his or her colleagues, and third was the mentor. They then continued to the next question, proceeding step by step to complete all five questions/steps for learning from the problem and then all five steps for learning from the success.

TABLE 6.1 Five-Step Reflection Format for Learning From Problems or for Learning From Both Problems and Successes

REFLECTION STEP	LEARNING FROM PROBLEMS	LEARNING FROM SUCCESSES
1. Identify a problematic or successful teaching experience/event that took place during your lesson so that it can be used for collective learning. (The preservice teacher is asked to provide a concise description of the relevant situation before and after the event selected for analysis.)		
2. Reconstruct your concrete actions that led to the outcomes. (The preservice teacher is repeatedly challenged to go beyond standard professional jargon and reconnect with the specific actions that led to the problematic or successful outcome.)		
3. Identify critical turning points. (The preservice teacher breaks down the steps that led to problematic or successful outcomes into chronologically ordered stages marked by turning points or milestones.)		
4. Craft principles of action based on your problematic/successful actions. (The preservice teacher is asked to form *principles of action*—abstractions based on the details of each specific event but general enough to be reflected upon in other educational contexts or by other educational staff.)		
5. Identify issues for further reflection and exploration. (The preservice teacher is invited to note issues for further reflection that could assure the open-ended nature of the learning process.)		

NOTE: All four research groups received a column to write their learning-from-problems steps of reflection. Only the *P+S* and *P+S+Peers* groups also received a column to write their learning-from-successes steps of reflection.

online resources ⟍ Available for download from https://resources.corwin.com/WisdomofPractice

P+S group (n = 30). Each preservice teacher in this group deliberated on a problematic event and then went on to deliberate on a successful event from the lesson he or she had just taught, but only with the mentor who had observed the lesson. Using the first question in the five-step reflection format, the preservice teacher reflected first, then the mentor. The two of them then continued to the next question and thus proceeded to complete all five steps for learning from the problem and then all five steps for learning from the success.

P+Peers group (n = 34). Each preservice teacher in this group deliberated solely on a problematic event from the lesson he or she had just taught, together with the mentor and three preservice colleagues who had observed the lesson. Using the first question in the five-step reflection format, the preservice teacher reflected first, followed by peers' reflections, and finally by the mentor's reflection. They then continued to the next question and thus proceeded to complete all five steps for learning from the problem.

P group (n = 29). Each preservice teacher in this group deliberated solely on a problematic event from the lesson he or she had just taught, with only the mentor who had observed the lesson. Using the first question in the five-step reflection format, the preservice teacher reflected first, followed by the mentor's reflection. The two of them proceeded to the next question and thus completed all five steps for learning from the problem.

Results indicated greater performance improvement on pedagogical content-knowledge measures (comprehending, designing, and teaching) and on sense of self-efficacy measures (personal science teaching efficacy and science teaching outcome expectancy) when contemplating both problematic and successful experiences than when focusing solely on problematic experiences. Interestingly, the *P+S* group (inquiring into problems and successes with the mentor alone) revealed significantly higher correlations between the pedagogical content knowledge components and the self-efficacy components than the *P+Peers* group (inquiring into problems only but with the added input of analyzing aloud together with peer preservice teachers, under the mentor's guidance). Although we formulated no explicit assumption about the comparative effectiveness of the solo versus collective approaches due to the paucity of research in this area, we suggested that integrating both learning from problems and learning from successes as reflective frameworks in teacher education may develop important reciprocal processes between attitudes, knowledge, and behavior. In other words, whereas it is well-established that peer discourse and collective reflection help preservice teachers to develop their capacity to consider new perspectives, the current instructional/reflective framework of integrating both learning from problems and learning from successes may serve as better leverage for developing preservice teachers' capacities (attitudes, knowledge, and behaviors) to meet the growing challenges of today's schoolwork. This study's findings reframe the learning-from-problem focus, thus advising that the instructional framework of teacher education programs should carefully include learning from success, too. To illustrate, excerpts from the five-step reflection format featuring both problematic and successful experiences in teacher education are presented in Table 6.2.

TABLE 6.2 Five-Step Reflective Analysis of a Physics Lesson on Newton's Law: Reflection Format Featuring Both Problematic and Successful Experiences

	EXCERPTS	
REFLECTION STEP	LEARNING FROM PROBLEMS	LEARNING FROM SUCCESSES
1. **Identify a problematic or successful teaching experience/event that took place during your lesson so that it can be used for collective learning.** (The preservice teacher is asked to provide a concise description of the relevant situation before and after the event selected for analysis.)	⋏ After learning to solve problems in the context we were discussing (Newton's first law), the students didn't succeed in solving the first question. They gave up and were afraid to continue the learning activity.	⋏ At the beginning of the lesson, I estimated that 40% of students held misconceptions in the subject being learned (Newton's first law), while at the end of the lesson, only 5% gave incorrect answers.
2. **Reconstruct your concrete actions that led to the outcomes.** (The preservice teacher is repeatedly challenged to go beyond standard professional jargon and reconnect with the specific actions that led to the problematic or successful outcome.)	⋏ I explained the subject without demonstrating the process of problem solving. ⋏ The first exercise in the workbook was too complicated and difficult for the students.	⋏ At the outset of the lesson, I asked students to say what they knew or had heard about Newton's first law. ⋏ After reading the text, students deliberated on the subject, based on the guidelines that I had provided for them.
3. **Identify critical turning points.** (The preservice teacher breaks down the steps that led to the problematic or successful outcomes into chronologically ordered stages marked by turning points or milestones.)	⋏ I switched too quickly from explaining the idea to the practical phase of problem solving. ⋏ I hardly invested any time in demonstrating problem solving.	⋏ I started the lesson by eliciting students' prior knowledge. ⋏ We read the text and deliberated on various perceptions in a nonthreatening atmosphere.

(Continued)

TABLE 6.2 (Continued)

| REFLECTION STEP | EXCERPTS | |
	LEARNING FROM PROBLEMS	LEARNING FROM SUCCESSES
4. **Craft principles of action based on your problematic/successful actions.** (The preservice teacher is asked to form *principles of action*—abstractions based on the details of each specific event but general enough to be reflected upon in other educational contexts or by other educational staff.)	⋀ It is important to continuously evaluate whether the lesson's goals are met, not only at the end of the lesson. ⋀ Student-teacher dialogue needs to be based on students' prior knowledge and abilities. ⋀ It is important to provide better support for the bridging between the declarative phase and the procedural phase during the lesson.	⋀ Correcting misconceptions with regard to complex topics includes several critical stages: eliciting students' existing perceptions on the topic being studied, creating a cognitive dissonance between these perceptions and a new one, and deliberating on and exercising the new or different perception. ⋀ Changing students' perceptions requires an open, welcoming, and nonthreatening learning atmosphere.
5. **Identify issues for further reflection and exploration.** (The preservice teacher is invited to note issues for further reflection that could assure the open-ended nature of the learning process.)	⋀ What shall I do if I see during the practice phase that half of the students are performing well while the other half needs a major review? ⋀ What are other means that can be used for enhancing students' sense of self-efficacy in the process of learning complex constructs/subjects?	⋀ What can I do with students who do not like working in learning groups? ⋀ What can I do with advanced students who get bored during these learning activities?

NOTE: Excerpts from Schechter & Michalsky, 2014.

In sum, this study examined learning from problems and learning from successes as tools that could be implemented during the training of preservice teachers to help them acquire analytical self-reflection skills that could serve them in their in-service careers by working to improve their pedagogical content knowledge and their teaching self-efficacy in real-time future classrooms. Next, we decided to expand our empirical scrutiny of these two learning frameworks for additional important aspects of teacher education.

For example, using the same quasi-experimental design, we integrated systematic learning from problematic and successful experiences into teachers' preparatory programs (Michalsky & Schechter, 2013) with a focus on investigating how such learning would affect preservice physics teachers' capacity to teach self-regulated learning (SRL) to students. Specifically, SRL is considered an active process referring to "self-generated thoughts, feelings, and actions that are planned and cyclically adapted to the attainment of personal goals" (Zimmerman, 2000, p. 14). SRL involves a combination of cognitive, metacognitive, and motivational processes used in a learning context (Pintrich, 2000; Zimmerman, 2008). Interestingly, the results of our teacher education experiment favored joint learning from problems and successes over problem-only focused learning. Table 6.3 presents excerpts from these preservice physics teachers' post-teaching analysis sessions using the five-step reflection format as part of their teacher education program.

This study demonstrated that those preservice teachers who had contemplated both problematic and successful experiences improved more, not only in their actual teaching of SRL strategies to their students but also in the extent to which they actually arranged SRL-promoting learning environments for their students, in comparison to preservice teachers who contemplated only problematic experiences. Thus, the findings of this study helped support the value of incorporating success-based learning into teacher education training procedures, which were traditionally based on analyzing problems in order to improve teacher trainees' actual ability to teach their students the important SRL skills that have been highlighted as crucial for 21st-century learners.

In another recent study on how learning from successes and problems might be valuable in teacher education, we again integrated systematic collaborative learning from problematic and successful experiences into teachers' preparatory programs (Michalsky & Schechter, 2018). This time, we wanted to examine how such learning would be associated with additional important aspects of preservice physics teachers' functioning. Specifically, we investigated their (a) beliefs about SRL-teaching/learning pedagogies, (b) SRL-teaching self-efficacy (their beliefs about their own ability to teach SRL in the classroom), and (c) skills for designing an SRL-based lesson.

Results of this study indicated that preservice teachers who contemplated both problematic and successful experiences functioned better on all three of the measures that we assessed in comparison to those preservice teachers who

TABLE 6.3 Five-Step Reflective Analysis of an Introductory Physics Lesson: Reflection Format Featuring Both Problematic and Successful Experiences

REFLECTION STEP	EXCERPTS	
	LEARNING FROM PROBLEMS	LEARNING FROM SUCCESSES
1. **Identify a problematic or successful teaching experience/event that took place during your lesson so that it can be used for collective learning.** (The preservice teacher is asked to provide a concise description of the relevant situation before and after the events selected for analysis.)	⋏ While teaching, I did not check students' understanding of the learning process. The students didn't succeed in solving the first question. They gave up and were afraid to continue the learning activity.	⋏ I taught the subject gradually, providing students with easy questions, then more challenging ones. This helped students understand the subject, and it motivated them to continue taking an active role in the classroom discussion.
2. **Reconstruct your concrete actions that led to the outcomes.** (The preservice teacher is repeatedly challenged to go beyond standard professional jargon and reconnect with the specific actions that led to the problematic or successful outcome.)	⋏ I gave the students instructions without explaining: What is the name of the strategy I used? When do I generally use this strategy and why use it at all?	⋏ While teaching, I stopped and introduced the students to SRL strategies: While working on this kind of task, you should always ask yourself, *What do I already know?* and *What am I seeking?*
3. **Identify critical turning points.** (The preservice teacher breaks down the steps that led to problematic or successful outcomes into chronologically ordered stages marked by turning points or milestones.)	⋏ I did not explain what I was doing, why I was doing it, and when we need to do it. ⋏ I didn't allow enough students to talk about their difficulties in solving the exercise.	⋏ I started the lesson by eliciting students' three SRL strategies for solving physics problems. ⋏ Raising students' prior SRL knowledge took place in a forthcoming environment where every response was legitimate.

	EXCERPTS	
REFLECTION STEP	LEARNING FROM PROBLEMS	LEARNING FROM SUCCESSES
4. Craft principles of action based on your problematic/successful actions. (The preservice teacher is asked to form *principles of action*—abstractions based on the details of each specific event but general enough to be reflected upon in other educational contexts or by other educational staff.)	⋏ The teacher must think out loud more often and tell students what he or she is doing, how to use a specific strategy, when to use it, and how often it should be used. ⋏ It is imperative to construct a productive dialogue between teacher and students as a means of developing students' learning and understanding skills.	⋏ Students must be given some information about the meaning and importance of the SRL strategy, which enhances students' use of a particular tool when faced with subsequent similar problems, thereby contributing to their application of the strategy in appropriate settings. Teachers should explain clearly and provide examples of the use of self-regulation, especially for struggling students.
5. Identify issues for further reflection and exploration. (The preservice teacher is invited to note issues for further reflection that could assure the open-ended nature of the learning process.)	⋏ How can I perform more thinking aloud during the lesson? ⋏ What can I do to switch from my teacher's perspective to a student's perspective?	⋏ What can I do to adapt my teaching to students with different capabilities of self-regulation? ⋏ What can I do to motivate students during these learning activities?

NOTE: Excerpts from Michalsky & Schechter, 2013.

contemplated only problematic experiences. First, those who had analyzed both successes and problems tended to favor more student-centered learning than teacher-centered learning, which showed their awareness of the importance for students to self-construct their own knowledge (in SRL-promoting teaching methods) rather than being spoon-fed material by teachers (via frontal knowledge-transmission methods). In addition, the preservice teachers who had been trained to scrutinize both problems and successes that had arisen in their own physics teaching expressed stronger beliefs in their own ability to teach SRL to their students compared to their peers who had only focused on their lesson's problematic aspects. Finally, those preservice teachers who had learned how to think about what worked well in their lessons (not only what went wrong) were able to develop better SRL-based designs for teaching future physics lessons.

The traditional instructional approach to teacher education based on the rational–technical model of knowledge generation has been criticized as inappropriate for developing preservice teachers' understanding of how theory unfolds in the actual world. Scholars have urged university-based programs to develop a more practical orientation by allowing preservice teachers opportunities to learn about real-life problems (e.g., Diem & Carpenter, 2013). To bridge this theory–practice gap, learning from problems has been applied quite extensively in teacher preparatory programs around the world, especially in North America. The findings from the three studies outlined above reframe the learning-from-problem focus, thus calling on teacher educators to reinterpret the instructional framework of teacher education programs to include learning from success as well. Teacher educators' deliberate choice to integrate preservice teachers' learning from their own problematic and successful practices may nurture the practical wisdom necessary for these trainees to work effectively when they are hired to teach in dynamic school contexts. Thus, the findings described above suggest that teacher preparatory programs should consider switching cognitive gears between learning from problems and learning from successes.

PRINCIPAL PREPARATION

> The approach of learning from both problems and successes, which was absolutely new to me, was also really significant for me. Yes, we do things successfully, but we don't learn from them to help see how to succeed in our later tasks. Not everyone could comfortably hear about others' success; however, I acquired an important tool here of deriving lessons from previous success to use when I encounter future challenges. Now I understand that learning only from unsuccessful processes and events is a unidimensional approach, which is not enough for the complexity of school reality.
>
> —an aspiring preservice principal

The notion of combining learning from problems with learning from successes holds implications not only for teachers but also for school leaders. The approach that is most commonly applied during collaborative learning in contemporary principal preparation programs is one that continues to deal predominantly with learning from problems. Yet, such an approach may be seen as covering only some of the wide range of school situations. Ignoring a considerable part of the school leadership reality, namely all of the positive and successful practices that occur every day in these environments, may afford aspiring principals with a smaller number of strategies than they could have had at their disposal had they related to learning from successes as well. As an alternative to this prevalent framework for collaborative learning, it would be advisable to explore a broader approach, where aspiring principals integrate learning from problems as well as learning from successes.

To this end, a study was designed to explore a group of 24 aspiring principals who integrated learning from problems and learning from successes during a major seminar in their university-based leadership preparation program (Shaked & Schechter, 2018). The aspiring principals' perceptions regarding this integration as a framework for collaborative learning were the focus of the study. Qualitative data analysis showed that these aspiring principals attributed three main benefits to the integration of learning from problems and from successes. These three benefits are presented along with excerpts from aspiring principals:

1. *Seeing the whole picture.* The first benefit of joint learning from problems and successes may be seen as representing a more all-inclusive or comprehensive form of collaborative learning, which provides a broader view on the full range of school practices.

> I believe that the combination of learning from problems and learning from successes provides us with a more holistic mode of drawing conclusions out of various and frequently conflicting school practices.

2. *Exploring and making the best of school practices.* The second benefit of joint learning from problems and successes may be seen as representing greater accuracy in collaborative learning, which facilitates recognition and preservation of effective practices.

> The two different methods of learning from success and learning from problems complement each other because they show us not only the things that we need to do differently but also the good things that we have to learn from and continue doing.

3. *Drawing conclusions nonjudgmentally.* The third benefit of joint learning from problems and successes may be seen as representing a less daunting form of collaborative learning, which is done in a matter-of-fact, accepting manner.

> If we were to draw conclusions not only when something goes wrong but also when something works properly, then the meaning of drawing conclusions could be different for us. It could be done in a businesslike way, without the unpleasant feelings that arise when we learn from our problems, as we've experienced in the past.

In the context of principal preparation, these findings should be seen from two perspectives. First, the ways in which existing preparation programs train principals are a source of concern among various stakeholders (Anderson & Reynolds, 2015; Wallace Foundation, 2016). Researchers have criticized principal preparation programs for failing to adequately train prospective educational leaders for their roles, claiming that these programs do not produce qualified principals who are capable of running schools successfully (Darling-Hammond, Meyerson, La Pointe, & Orr, 2010; Schechter, 2011; Williams, 2015). To prepare aspiring principals for their future roles more effectively, some preparation programs employ collaborative analyses of cases taken from school reality (Weiler & Cray, 2012). Findings from the current study suggest that collaborative learning that solely analyzes problematic situations may be insufficient. The integration of learning from problems and learning from successes may be a satisfactory framework for collaborative learning in principal preparation programs because it is more holistic, more accurate, and less daunting than learning from problems alone.

Second, reflection on both problematic and successful pedagogical and administrative experiences can foster effective learning and interpretation systems— places and spaces where educators can ponder and cross-validate different perceptions of the same data. These inter-negotiations of beliefs and opinions regarding both problematic and successful professional practices may nurture multiple perspectives, consequently stimulating more holistic insights concerning schoolwork. Thus, switching cognitive gears between learning from problems and learning from successes can be an important mechanism for better sensemaking of school experiences (Ellis, Mendel, & Nir, 2006; Schechter, 2008). Integrating learning from problems with learning from successes in leadership preparation enables comparison, categorization, and exploration, leading to a learning process that can promote deep relational learning and the development of more complex and holistic explanations (Kurtz, Boukrina, & Gentner, 2013).

FURTHER INTEGRATION OF LEARNING FROM SUCCESSES AND PROBLEMS

As advocated earlier in this book, the identification of unresolved issues near the end of a learning process is a crucial stage in helping learners to reflect on various barriers, by-products, difficulties, and disappointments—some subjective and others objective. Thus, as a cornerstone for effective learning, issues for further study may also reveal a series of diverging paths leading to further individual and group learning. In this vein, as we near the end of this book, I next explore as-yet uncharted territory in the area of blending learning from problems with learning from successes.

Despite the series of research studies exploring teachers' and principals' actual application of an approach to collective learning that shifts gears between a focus on problems and a focus on successes, questions remain regarding this innovative approach. Can learning from successes and problems serve as a link between school restructuring efforts and innovations at the classroom level? What are the connections between systemic processes of learning from success and learning from problems on the one hand and teachers' outcomes such as job commitment or job satisfaction on the other hand? How might systemic processes of shifting gears between learning from problems and learning from successes be related to actual student outcomes such as scholastic achievements, engagement levels, and well-being?

Similarly, as different teachers do not necessarily share the same beliefs and values about what is successful or not, one teacher's perceived success may be another's perceived failure. When participants classify their colleagues' experiences into categories of either *successful* or *unsuccessful*, it is the obligation of the learning coordinator to uncover the potentially rich information residing within each experience. This triggers the question: In order to cope with the unintended possible division between "successful" and "unsuccessful" teachers in a given group, can learning coordinators serve as gatekeepers for any dispositional ideology while empowering teachers to authentically share what they perceive as their successful and challenging practices?

In addition to developing structural arrangements for learning, school leaders need to encourage teachers to collectively explore both their successful and problematic practices, acknowledging faculty members as creative partners for joint learning ventures. Therefore, institutionalizing forums for collective learning from successes and problems in schools needs to be supported by a specifically designed learning culture. Without sufficient emphasis on this sort of learning culture (which aims to embody trust, generosity, and transparency), even the best-intentioned learning mechanisms based on social learning processes can paradoxically reinforce stereotypical thinking, support the status quo, and reproduce existing norms and practices (Printy, 2008; Wenger, 1998).

In particular, two main sets of issues remain unexplored regarding the value of learning from both successes and problems as a catalyst for growth and change: issues related to teacher training and induction and issues related to policy implementation. These issues are explored next.

FURTHER ISSUES FOR TEACHER TRAINING AND INDUCTION

Problem-based learning is gaining momentum in various professional training programs such as business administration, psychology, law, and social work. Teacher training programs around the world also tend to be based on problem-solving learning methods for the professional development of those who will be teaching children and to help teachers better link theoretical material with the realities of day-to-day school life. Although problem-based learning for prospective teachers is a positive development compared to the traditional approach of frontal lectures for the transmission of predefined pedagogical knowledge, it cannot be considered a constructivist approach to teacher instruction. One of the main claims against the overuse of the problem-solving method is that it focuses on reducing burdens and stress and takes place only within the boundaries of familiar and common situations. If so, it is important to examine learning from successes as another complementary way for developing preservice teachers, especially when helping teacher trainees create a pedagogical and professional identity.

The transition from the status of a preservice teacher to that of a new teacher in a school is sudden. This transition entails many difficulties, such as organizational loneliness, anxiety, severe stress, loss of self-confidence, and doubts as to personal ability. These difficulties may lead novice teachers to adapt passively to the system, to avoid utilization of new teaching strategies, or to rigidly harden into conservative behavior patterns—which are all incompatible with effective teaching. It is therefore necessary for teacher educators to carefully examine whether the combination of learning from problems and learning from success during teachers' field internship stages may provide an answer to the emotional and psychological characteristics of the entry phase of the teaching job. It is possible that integration of these joint, complementary frameworks at the preservice preparation stage may enable novice teachers to focus more effectively on teaching and administrative areas of their work.

Clearly, follow-up research should be conducted to examine how interns' training systems, whether those within a school (teacher/mentor, principal) or those outside schools (academic courses that include analysis of events) can be aided by the philosophy and strategy of learning from success. When conducting such research, some questions could serve as a focus: How can learning from success serve the teacher trainee's mentor (who is also a teacher or principal) in performing formative evaluation processes? What is the role of learning from success (and learning from problems) in the internship workshops in colleges and universities? Is being on the lookout for successes (even the smallest), especially a joint analysis of the factors that led to their occurrence, likely to help novice teachers overcome the difficulties of initiation into the system?

FURTHER ISSUES CONCERNING POLICY IMPLEMENTATION

Educational systems worldwide are replete with policy-driven (top-down) school reform efforts. These school reforms generally come as a response to a perceived crisis and/or problem. As such, these top-down reforms often do not have a significant impact on school life, as they tend to offer quick-fixes to the problems within the existing political frameworks of policymakers. Nevertheless, reform efforts that evolve from practitioners' analyses of their own successes can tighten the link between policymakers' agendas and practitioners' work, encouraging both to collaboratively build upon emerging successes as leverage for accountability-mandated school improvement and turnaround. Can joint learning from success, coupled with learning from problems, better link educators' practices at the school level with top-down reform models?

Policy-driven reform efforts identify teachers' and leaders' sensemaking as a collective endeavor (Coburn, 2016; Ganon-Shilon & Schechter, 2017, 2019; Schechter & Shaked, 2017). *Sensemaking* is an ongoing process through which people work to understand issues or events that create ambiguities in routines in which they are involved (Maitlis & Christianson, 2014). It is an active process of constructing meaning from concurrent stimuli, mediated by prior knowledge, experiences, beliefs, and values that are embedded in the social context within which people work. When individuals encounter moments of uncertainty, as manifested in cases of top-down reform initiatives, they frame their environment through an interpretive mental model to make sense of what has occurred (Smerek, 2011; Sumbera, Pazey, & Lashley, 2014; Weick, 2009). Through multiple interpretations of the ambiguous event, individuals develop their initial sense of the situation into a more integrated one. In this sense, several questions should be posed regarding sensemaking of educational policies: How can educators' learning from their own successful and problematic events construct new meaning from the ambiguous school experiences imposed by top-down reforms? More importantly, can a shared sensemaking process be envisioned among teachers, principals, superintendents, and policymakers regarding schools' successes and problematic experiences, which may be in better keeping with today's rapidly changing educational reform scene?

Conclusion

Let's Start Our Journey

Enacting Educators' Successful Wisdom of Practice

> Learning from success requires work. Reflecting on successes and deciding that we want to learn from them entail struggles and efforts. This is its major disadvantage—it requires work. We tend to jump as if bitten by a snake when encountering failures, but if something is all right, we just say, "It was nice." This is a habit that requires mental work. If we already succeeded in finishing a certain assignment, why do we need to invest work in analyzing exactly what in it was successful? This requires a change in cultural perception.
>
> —a high school principal

Teachers often feel that most of their professional conduct evolves as a consequence of an endless repetition of experiences of handling and focusing on how to fix malfunctions, breakdowns, or crises. Rare is the occasion when schools stop to look at what went right; instead, the common voices overheard in school hallways and teacher lounges are those reacting to or complaining about what went wrong. Obviously, when critical situations are occurring in real time and children are involved, it is the utmost responsibility of all those involved to ensure the best outcomes possible, and this often requires an unvarnished straight-on solution to pressing problems. However, this is not to say that schools should not take an occasional step back from the everyday mayhem to learn how to do things better. It is during these important learning situations, which all schools should implement as a habit of practice, that the question arises as to how to best help teachers and principals improve not only their outcomes but also their ability to continue learning more and more effectively.

Unfortunately, the focus on learning solely from problems that has predominated teachers' learning experiences in schools to date is a biased viewpoint that encourages despair among both educators and students. Looking only at what went wrong prevents both sides from overcoming this despair and reaching a place where there is hope. When educational staff learns mainly from limitations and not from possibilities, efforts to seek success as a source of learning and development are avoided.

This book has brought theory and evidence to demonstrate that learning from success can render a genuine change in schools. Learning from success has the power to transform teachers' discourse about their practice. In essence, the formalization of learning-from-success forums within a school or school system can generate commitment to and investment in reflective learning among diverse members of a school community. This potential is inherent to such learning-from-success forums for several reasons:

1. The search for and focus on successes of school members frequently calls attention to a range of positive processes that had previously gone relatively unnoticed. Recognizing and learning from these activities reaffirms a connectedness with the school's vision and its mission, which awakens a sense of professional pride and competence.

2. The identification of success in important areas of activity that previously had elicited a great degree of frustration and helplessness revitalizes stakeholders' investment in these areas. Thus, teachers' capacity to generate actionable knowledge broadens the scope of success-based work in the school.

3. An act of learning, which essentially is "search and reflection," demands cooperation among a variety of stakeholders both at the school level (teachers, nonteaching staff, students, and parents) and outside the school (professionals in a wide variety of frameworks such as welfare services, etc.). Inevitably, learning that is based on cooperation and partnership creates an atmosphere of reciprocity, which removes hierarchical barriers that tend to bar joint organizational learning ventures.

4. Constructing learning processes through advancement of learning-from-success forums transforms the experience of learning and discovery into an organic component of a system's modes of operation. In this way, learning from success augments staff members' ability to initiate independent learning and creates a culture of openness to learning.

5. The school learning process becomes a catalyst for the development of new leadership within the school and in related systems. Because the learners are partners in the creation of knowledge, they become its disseminators as well as the initiators of new knowledge-based work methods both within and outside the school.

It takes considerable individual maturity and a deliberately fostered collegiate system for organizational members to remain open to learning while discussing their problems or failures with colleagues. In such settings, a tendency toward defensiveness often prevails. It is easier to be forthcoming with colleagues when retrospectively reflecting upon achievements. Indeed, continuing to be forthcoming with colleagues when reflecting upon achievements, which in turn builds trust, becomes a resource that enhances practitioners' capacity to learn in the future, even in highly threatening circumstances. Thus, groups would do well to begin embarking on their collective retrospective learning journey with a focus on group members' successes before moving on to analyzing members' problems or failures. Eventually, after acquiring the skills for open-minded peer questioning and systematic inquiry into successes, group participants will be more ready to juggle their mindsets and integrate both learning from successes and learning from problems.

Although learning from success has been perceived as the enemy of experimentation and innovation, this book has systematically presented its teacher-friendly benefits and advantages, as supported by research and accompanied by practical guidelines and tools for the advocated development teams and multistep inquiry process. Collective learning about successes in schools offers an impressive potential for empowering teachers' own grassroots strengths by tapping teachers as a precious bottom-up resource that already exists and thrives within the school, instead of turning to external sources such as governmental policymakers to impose top-down educational reforms. Yet, teacher and principal preparation programs and, of course, school leaders must make a deliberate choice to integrate continuous collective learning from teachers' problematic and successful practices in order to nurture the practical wisdom necessary to work in dynamic school contexts.

Schools that truly learn are those that enact their educators' professional successes as a catalyst for ongoing learning to confront challenging situations in everyday school life. Professional educators who protest the global prevalence of a negative atmosphere in their schools will appreciate a shift toward learning from their own successes, which should be their approach in their classrooms to build a positive future together with students. When considering education systems' predominant worldwide focus (aligned with human predispositions) on ways to correct what went wrong, the learning-from-success model is a paradigm shift that will require a retooling of activities, thinking, and actions within continuous improvement cycles and turnaround efforts. Hopefully, this book has empowered practitioners with the tools and understanding necessary to undertake this transformational shift and embark on the exciting journey of nurturing the remarkable wisdom of practice characterizing those educators who craft magical learning moments with our children day by day.

References

PREFACE

Argyris, C., & Schon, D. (1996). *Organizational learning II: Theory, method and practice.* Reading, MA: Addison-Wesley.

Bach, R. (1970). *Jonathan Livingston—Seagull.* New York, NY: The Macmillan Company.

Blackmore, J. (2006). Deconstructing diversity discourses in the field of educational management and leadership. *Educational Management Administration & Leadership, 34*(2), 181–199.

Darling-Hammond, L., Meyerson, D., La Pointe, M., & Orr, M. T. (2010). *Preparing principals for a changing world: Lessons from effective school leadership programs.* San Francisco, CA: Jossey-Bass.

DuFour, R., & DuFour, R. (2013). *Learning by doing: A handbook for professional learning communities at work.* Bloomington, IN: Solution Tree Press.

Fullan, M. (2014). *The principal: Three keys to maximizing impact.* San Francisco, CA: Jossey-Bass.

Fullan, M. (2016). *Indelible leadership: Always leave them learning.* Thousand Oaks, CA: Corwin.

Giles, C., & Hargreaves, A. (2006). The sustainability of schools as learning organizations and professional learning communities during standard-based reform. *Educational Administration Quarterly, 42*(1), 124–156.

Hargreaves, A., & Fullan, M. (2012). *Professional capital: Transforming teaching in every school.* New York, NY: Teachers College Press.

Hord, S. M. (2016). Learning together for leading together. Reach the highest standard in professional learning. *Leadership, 37.*

Learning Forward: The Professional Learning Association. (2018). *Standards for professional learning.* Oxford, OH: Author.

Louis, K. S. (2006). Changing the culture of schools: Professional community, organizational learning, and trust. *Journal of School Leadership, 16*(5), 477–489.

Lu, J., & Hallinger, P. (2018). A mirroring process: From school management team cooperation to teacher collaboration. *Leadership and Policy in Schools, 17*(2), 238–263.

Mulford, B., & Silins, H. (2011). Revised models and conceptualization of successful school principalship that improve student outcomes. *International Journal of Educational Management, 25*(1), 61–82.

Organization for Economic Co-operation and Development [OECD]. (2016). *Education at a glance 2016: OECD indicators.* Paris, France: Author. Retrieved from http://www.oecd.org/edu/education-at-a-glance-19991487.htm

Ravitch, D. (2014). *Reign of errors: The hoax of the privatization movement and the danger to America's public schools.* New York, NY: Vintage.

Rosenfeld, J. M. (1997). Learning from success: How to design social work to be suitable for its purposes. *Social Welfare, 17*(4), 261–281.

Rosenfeld, J. M., Schon, D. A., & Sykes, I. J. (1995). *Out from under: Lessons from projects for inaptly served children and families.* Jerusalem, Israel: Brookdale.

Schechter, C. (2010). Learning from success as a leverage for professional learning community: Exploring a school improvement process. *Teachers College Record, 112*(1), 180–224.

Schechter, C. (2011b). Switching cognitive gears: Problem-based learning and success-based learning as an instructional framework in leadership education. *Journal of Educational Administration, 49*(2), 143–165.

Schechter, C. (2011c). Towards communal negotiation of meaning in schools: Principals' perceptions of collective learning from success. *Teachers College Record, 113*(11), 2415–2459.

Schechter, C. (2012). The professional learning community as perceived by school superintendents, principals, and teachers. *International Review of Education, 58*(6), 717–734.

Schleicher, A. (2012). *Preparing teachers and developing school leaders for the 21st century: Lessons from around the world.* Paris, France: OECD.

Taylor, F. W. (1911). *The principles of scientific management.* New York, NY: Harper and Brothers.

Chapter 1

Andrews, D., & Crowther, F. (2006). Teachers as leaders in a knowledge society: Encouraging signs of a new professionalism. *Journal of School Leadership, 16*(5), 535–549.

Bolam, R., McMahon, A., Stoll, L., Thomas, S., & Wallace, M. (2005). *Creating and sustaining effective professional learning communities.* Research Report 637. Bristol, England: Department for Education and Skills, University of Bristol.

Bryk, A. S., Camburn, E., & Louis, K. S. (1999). Professional community in Chicago elementary schools: Facilitating factors and organizational consequences. *Educational Administration Quarterly, 35*(5), 751–781.

Chaplin, C. (Director). (1936). *Modern times* [Motion Picture]. New York, NY: United Artists.

Collinson, V., & Cook, T. F. (2007). *Organizational learning: Improving learning, teaching, and leading in school systems.* Thousand Oaks, CA: SAGE.

De Neve, D., Devos, G., & Tuytens, M. (2015). The importance of job resources and self-efficacy for beginning teachers' professional learning in differentiated instruction. *Teaching and Teacher Education, 47*, 30–41.

Dogan, S., Pringle, R., & Mesa, J. (2016). The impacts of professional learning communities on science teachers' knowledge, practice and student learning: A review. *Professional Development in Education, 42*(4), 569–588.

Drago-Severson, E., Roy, P., & Frank, V. (2016). *Reach the highest standards in professional learning.* Thousand Oaks, CA: Corwin.

DuFour, R. (2004). What is a "professional learning community"? *Educational Leadership, 61*(8), 6–11.

DuFour, R., & DuFour, R. (2013). *Learning by doing: A handbook for professional learning communities at work*. Bloomington, IN: Solution Tree.

DuFour, R., Eaker, R., & Many, T. (2006). *Learning by doing: A handbook for professional learning communities at work*. Bloomington, IN: Solution Tree.

Fullan, M. (2016). *Indelible leadership: Always leave them learning*. Thousand Oaks, CA: Corwin.

Giles, C., & Hargreaves, A. (2006). The sustainability of schools as learning organizations and professional learning communities during standard-based reform. *Educational Administration Quarterly, 42*(1), 124–156.

Gray, J. A. (2011). *Professional learning communities and the role of enabling school structures and trust* (Order No. 3478583). Available from ProQuest Dissertations & Theses Global; Social Science Premium Collection. (903795176). Retrieved from https://libproxy.library.unt.edu/login?url=https://search.proquest.com/docview/903795176?accountid=7113

Gray, J. A., & Summers, R. (2015). International professional learning communities: The role of enabling school structures, trust, and collective efficacy. *International Education Journal: Comparative Perspectives, 14*(3), 61–75.

Greene, W. (2007). Building a professional learning community for teachers of Hebrew. *Jewish Education News*. Retrieved June 30, 2010, from http://caje.wikispaces.com/JEN+Article+Greene

Hargreaves, A., & Fullan, M. (2012). *Professional capital: Transforming teaching in every school*. New York, NY: Teachers College Press.

Hord, S. M. (2016). Learning together for leading together. Reach the highest standard in professional learning. *Leadership, 37*.

Hord, S. M., & Sommers, W. A. (2008). *Leading professional learning communities: Voices from research and practice*. Thousand Oaks, CA: Corwin.

Lee, J. C., Zhang, Z., & Yin, H. (2011). A multilevel analysis of the impact of a professional learning community, faculty trust in colleagues and collective efficacy on teacher commitment to students. *Teaching and Teacher Education, 27*(5), 820–830.

Louis, K. S. (2006). Changing the culture of schools: Professional community, organizational learning, and trust. *Journal of School Leadership, 16*(5), 477–489.

Mann, T. (1924). *The magic mountain*. Berlin, Germany: Fischer Verlag.

McLaughlin, M. W., & Talbert, J. E. (2006). *Building school-based teacher learning communities: Professional strategies to improve student achievement*. New York, NY: Teachers College Press.

Mitchell, C., & Sackney, L. (2006). Building schools, building people: The school principal's role in leading a learning community. *Journal of School Leadership, 16*(5), 627–639.

Mulford, B., & Silins, H. (2011). Revised models and conceptualization of successful school principalship that improve student outcomes. *International Journal of Educational Management, 25*(1), 61–82.

Opfer, V. D., & Pedder, D. (2011). Conceptualizing teacher professional learning. *Review of Educational Research, 81*(3), 376–407.

Park, M., & So, K. (2014). Opportunities and challenges for teacher professional development: A case of collaborative learning community in South Korea. *International Education Studies, 7*, 96–108.

Rosenholtz, S. J. (1989). *Teachers' workplace: The social organization of schools*. New York, NY: Teachers College Press.

Roy, P., & Hord, S. M. (2006). It's everywhere, but what is it? Professional learning communities. *Journal of School Leadership*, *16*(5), 490–501.

Schechter, C. (2010). Learning from success as a leverage for professional learning community: Exploring a school improvement process. *Teachers College Record*, *112*(1), 180–224.

Schechter, C. (2012). Developing teachers' collective learning: Collective learning from success as perceived by three echelons in the school system. *International Journal of Educational Research*, *56*, 60–74.

Schechter, C. (2018). Enacting President Trump's leadership contract with educators: Toward a communal leadership perspective. *Journal of Educational Administration and History*, *50*(1), 32–40.

Schmoker, M. (2004). Tipping point: From feckless reform to substantive instructional improvement. *Phi Delta Kappan*, *85*(6), 424–432.

Steyn, G. M. (2013). Building professional learning communities to enhance continuing professional development in South Africa schools. *Anthropologist*, *15*(3), 277–289.

Stoll, L., & Louis, K. S. (Eds.). (2007). *Professional learning communities: Divergence, depth and dilemmas*. London/New York: Open University Press/McGraw Hill.

Stoll, L., McMahon, A., & Thomas, S. (2006). Identifying and leading effective professional learning communities. *Journal of School Leadership*, *16*(5), 611–623.

Trust, T., & Horrocks, B. (2017). "I never feel alone in my classroom": Teacher professional growth within a blended community of practice. *Professional Development in Education*, *43*(4), 645–665.

Vangrieken, K., Meredith, C., Packer, T., & Kyndt, E. (2017). Teacher communities as a context for professional development: A systematic review. *Teaching and Teacher Education*, *61*, 47–59.

Veelen, R. V., Sleegers, P. J., & Endedijk, M. D. (2017). Professional learning among school leaders in secondary education: The impact of personal and work context factors. *Educational Administration Quarterly*, *53*(6), 16–25.

Vescio, V., Ross, D., & Adams, A. (2008). A review of research on the impact of professional learning communities on teaching practice and student learning. *Teaching and Teacher Education*, *24*(1), 80–91.

Vollenbroek, W., Wetterling, J., & de Vries, S. (2017). Professional communities of practice: We need them, but how to develop them successfully? In A. Marcus-Quinn & T. Hourigan (Eds.), *Handbook on digital learning for K–12 schools* (pp. 483–494). New York, NY: Springer International Publishing.

Wake, G., Swan, M., & Foster, C. (2016). Professional learning through the collaborative design of problem-solving lessons. *Journal of Mathematics Teacher Education*, *19*(3), 243–260.

CHAPTER 2

Argyris, C. (1993). *Knowledge for action: A guide to overcoming barriers to organizational change*. San Francisco, CA: Jossey-Bass.

Argyris, C., & Schon, D. (1996). *Organizational learning II: Theory, method and practice*. Reading, MA: Addison-Wesley.

Barber, W., King, S., & Buchanan, S. (2015). Problem based learning and authentic assessment in digital pedagogy: Embracing the role of collaborative communities. *Electronic Journal of e-Learning, 13*(2), 59–67.

Baumard, P., & Starbuck, W. H. (2005). Learning from failures: Why it may not happen. *Long Range Planning, 38*(3), 281–298.

Beaulieu, S., Roy, M., & Pasquero, J. (2002). *Linking the management of legitimacy and the learning process: Evidence from a case study*. Quebec, Canada: University of Sherbrooke.

Bierly, P. E., Kessler, E. H., & Christensen, E. W. (2000). Organizational learning, knowledge and wisdom. *Journal of Organizational Change Management, 13*(6), 595–618.

Brown, J. S., & Duguid, P. (1996). Organizational learning and communities of practice: Toward a unified view of working, learning, and innovation. In M. Cohen & L. Sproull (Eds.), *Organizational learning* (pp. 58–82). Thousand Oaks, CA: SAGE.

Bubsy, J. S. (1999). The effectiveness of collective retrospection as a mechanism of organizational learning. *The Journal of Applied Behavioral Science, 35*(1), 109–129.

Cameron, K., Dutton, J., & Quinn, R. (2003). *Positive organizational scholarship: Foundations of a new discipline*. San Francisco, CA: Berrett-Koehler.

Coperrider, D. L., Sorensen, P. F., & Whitney, D. (Eds.). (2000). *Appreciative inquiry: Rethinking human organization toward a positive theory of change*. Champaign, IL: Stipes.

Daft, R. L., & Weick, K. E. (1984). Toward a model of organizations as interpretation systems. *Academy of Management Review, 9*, 284–295.

De Neve, D., Devos, G., & Tuytens, M. (2015). The importance of job resources and self-efficacy for beginning teachers' professional learning in differentiated instruction. *Teaching and Teacher Education, 47*, 30–41.

Dewey, J. (1933). *How we think: A restatement of the relation of reflective thinking to the educative process*. Lexington, MA: Heath and Company.

Dillon, J. T. (1994). The questions of deliberation. In J. T. Dillon (Ed.), *Deliberation in education and society* (pp. 3–24). Norwood, NJ: Ablex.

Dodgson, M. (1993). Organizational learning: A review of some literatures. *Organization Studies, 14*(3), 375–394.

Edwards, S., & Hammer, M. (2006). Laura's story: Using problem based learning in early childhood and primary teacher education. *Teaching and Teacher Education, 22*, 465–477.

Elder, A. D. (2015). Using a brief form of problem-based learning in a research methods class: Perspectives of instructor and students. *Journal of University Teaching and Learning Practice, 12*(1), 1–12.

Ellis, S., & Davidi, I. (2005). After-event reviews: Drawing lessons from successful and failed events. *Journal of Applied Psychology, 90*(5), 857–871.

Ellis, S., Mendel, R., & Nir, M. (2006). Learning from successful and failed experiences: The moderating role of a kind of after-event review. *Journal of Applied Psychology, 91*(3), 669–680.

Feldman, J. (1989). On the difficulty of learning from experience. In H. P. Sims & D. A. Gioia (Eds.), *The thinking organization: Dynamics of organizational social cognition* (pp. 263–292). San Francisco, CA: Jossey-Bass.

Gino, F., & Pisano, G. P. (2011). Why leaders don't learn from success. *Harvard Business Review, 89*(4), 68–74.

Gouinlock, J. (1992). Dewey's theory of moral deliberation. In J. E. Tiles (Ed.), *John Dewey: Critical assessment* (pp. 218–228). New York, NY: Routledge.

Grimmett, P. P. (1988). The nature of reflection and Schon's conception in perspective. In P. P. Grimmett & G. L. Erickson (Eds.), *Reflection in teacher education* (pp. 5–16). New York, NY: Pacific Educational Press.

Halverson, R., Grigg, J., Prichett, R., & Thomas, C. (2005). *The new instructional leadership: Creating data-driven instructional systems in schools.* Paper presented at the Annual Meeting of the National Council of Professors of Educational Administration, Washington, DC.

Hoy, W., & Tarter, J. (2011). Positive psychology and educational administration: An optimistic research agenda. *Educational Administration Quarterly, 47*(3), 427–445.

Huber, G. P. (1996). Organizational learning: The contributing processes and the literatures. In M. D. Cohen & L. S. Sproull (Eds.), *Organizational learning* (pp. 124–162). Thousand Oaks, CA: SAGE.

Kolb, D. A. (1984). *Experiential learning: Experience as the source.* Englewood Cliffs, NJ: Prentice Hall.

Kruse, S. D. (2003). Remembering as organizational memory. *Journal of Educational Administration, 41*(4), 332–347.

Lant, T. K., & Mezias, S. J. (1992). An organizational learning model of convergence: A reorientation. *Organization Science, 3*(1), 47–71.

Launamma, P., & March, J. G. (1987). Adaptive coordination of a learning team. *Management Science, 33*, 107–123.

Le Cornu, R., & Ewing, R. (2008). Reconceptualising professional experiences in pre-service teacher education: Reconstructing the past to embrace the future. *Teaching and Teacher Education, 24*(7), 1799–1812.

Levitt, B., & March, J. (1996). Organizational learning. In M. D. Cohen & L. S. Sproull (Eds.), *Organizational learning* (pp. 516–540). Thousand Oaks, CA: SAGE.

Louis, K. S. (2006). Changing the culture of schools: Professional community, organizational learning, and trust. *Journal of School Leadership, 16*(5), 477–489.

Lundin, M., Öberg, P., & Josefsson, C. (2015). Learning from success: Are successful governments role models? *Public Administration, 93*(3), 733–752.

Madsen, P. M., & Desai, V. (2010). Failing to learn? The effects of failure and success on organizational learning in the global orbital launch vehicle industry. *Academy of Management Journal, 53*(3), 451–476.

Mahenswaran, D., & Chaiken, S. (1991). Promoting systematic processing in low-motivation settings: Effects of incongruent information on processing and judgment. *Journal of Personality and Social Psychology, 61*, 13–25.

March, J. (1996). Exploration and exploitation in organizational learning. In M. D. Cohen & L. S. Sproull (Eds.), *Organizational learning* (pp. 101–123). Thousand Oaks, CA: SAGE.

Marks, H. M., & Louis, S. K. (1999). Teacher empowerment and the capacity for organizational learning. *Educational Administration Quarterly, 35*(5), 707–750.

Michalsky, T., & Schechter, C. (2013). Preservice teachers' self-regulated learning: Integrating learning from problems and learning from successes. *Teaching and Teacher Education, 30*(1), 60–73.

Mulford, B., & Silins, H. (2011). Revised models and conceptualization of successful school principalship that improve student outcomes. *International Journal of Educational Management, 25*(1), 61–82.

Nilsson, W. (2015). Positive institutional work: Exploring institutional work through the lens of positive organizational scholarship. *Academy of Management Review*, *40*(3), 370–398.

Printy, S. (2008). Leadership for teacher learning: A community of practice perspective. *Educational Administration Quarterly*, *44*(2), 187–226.

Rosenfeld, J. M. (1997, September). *Learning from success: How to forge actionable knowledge for social work*. Opening lecture at the forum on learning from success. Alice Solomon Facchochschule, Berlin, Germany.

Rosenfeld, J. M., Schon, D. A., & Sykes, I. J. (1995). *Out from under: Lessons from projects for inaptly served children and families*. Jerusalem, Israel: Brookdale.

Rosenfeld, J. M., & Sykes, I. S. (1998). Toward "good enough" service to inaptly served families and children: Barriers and opportunities. *European Journal of Social Work*, *1*(3), 285–300.

Sabah, Y., & Rosenfeld, J. M. (2001). How can social welfare bureaus become learning organizations? *Journal of Social-Educational Work*, *15*, 143–162.

Schechter, C. (2008a). Organizational learning mechanisms: Its meaning, measure, and implications for school improvement. *Educational Administration Quarterly*, *44*(2), 155–186.

Schechter, C. (2010). Learning from success as a leverage for professional learning community: Exploring a school improvement process. *Teachers College Record*, *112*(1), 180–224.

Schechter, C. (2011b). Switching cognitive gears: Problem-based learning and success-based learning as an instructional framework in leadership education. *Journal of Educational Administration*, *49*(2), 143–165.

Schechter, C. (2011c). Towards communal negotiation of meaning in schools: Principals' perceptions of collective learning from success. *Teachers College Record*, *113*(11), 2415–2459.

Schechter, C. (2012). Developing teachers' collective learning: Collective learning from success as perceived by three echelons in the school system. *International Journal of Educational Research*, *56*, 60–74.

Schechter, C. (2013). Collective learning in schools: Exploring the perceptions of leadership trainees. *International Journal of Educational Management*, *27*(3), 273–291.

Schechter, C., & Atarchi, L. (2014). The meaning and measure of organizational learning mechanisms in secondary schools. *Educational Administration Quarterly*, *50*(4), 577–609.

Schechter, C., & Michalsky, T. (2014). Juggling our mindsets: Learning from success as a complementary instructional framework in teacher education. *Teachers College Record*, *116*(2), 1–48.

Schechter, C., Sykes, I., & Rosenfeld, J. (2004). Learning from success: A leverage for transforming schools into learning communities. *Planning and Changing*, *35*(3&4), 154–168.

Schechter, C., Sykes, I., & Rosenfeld, J. (2008). Learning from success as leverage for school learning: Lessons from a national program. *International Journal of Leadership in Education*, *11*(3), 301–318.

Schein, E. H. (1992). *Organizational culture and leadership*. San Francisco, CA: Jossey-Bass.

Schon, D. (1983). *The reflective practitioner*. New York, NY: Basic Books.

Schwab, J. (1978). The practical: A language for curriculum. In I. Westurby & N. J. Wilkof (Eds.), *Science, curriculum, and liberal education* (pp. 287–321). Chicago, IL: The University of Chicago Press.

Seligman, M. E. P., & Csikszentmihalyi, M. (2000). Positive psychology: An introduction. *American Psychologist, 25,* 3–14.

Senge, P. (2006). *The fifth discipline: The art and practice of the learning organization* (2nd ed.). New York, NY: Currency, Doubleday.

Sitkin, S. (1996). Learning through failure: The strategy of small losses. In M. D. Cohen & L. S. Sproull (Eds.), *Organizational learning* (pp. 541–578). Thousand Oaks, CA: SAGE.

Slavich, G. M., & Zimbardo, P. G. (2012). Transformation teaching: Theoretical underpinnings, basic principles, and core methods. *Educational Psychology Reviews, 24*(4), 569–608.

Sroufe, R., & Ramos, D. P. (2015). Leveraging collaborative, thematic problem-based learning to integrate curricula. *Decision Sciences Journal of Innovative Education, 13*(2), 151–176.

Virany, B., Tushman, M., & Romanelli, E. (1996). Executive succession and organization outcomes in turbulent environments: An organizational learning approach. In M. D. Cohen & L. S. Sproull (Eds.), *Organizational learning* (pp. 302–329). Thousand Oaks, CA: SAGE.

Walker, D. (1990). *Fundamentals of curriculum*. Orlando, FL: Harcourt Brace Jovanovich.

Weick, K. E. (1982). Administering education in loosely coupled schools. *Phi Delta Kappan, 63,* 673–676.

Whitney, D., & Fredrickson, B. L. (2015). Appreciative inquiry meets positive psychology. *AI Practitioner, 17*(3), 18–26.

CHAPTER 3

Argyris, C., & Schon, D. (1996). *Organizational learning II: Theory, method and practice*. Reading, MA: Addison-Wesley.

Giles, C., & Hargreaves, A. (2006). The sustainability of schools as learning organizations and professional learning communities during standard-based reform. *Educational Administration Quarterly, 42*(1), 124–156.

Goddard, R., Goddard, Y., Kim, E. S., & Miller, R. (2015). A theoretical and empirical analysis of the roles of instructional leadership, teacher collaboration, and collective efficacy beliefs in support of student learning. *American Journal of Education, 121*(4), 501–530.

Louis, K. S. (2006). Changing the culture of schools: Professional community, organizational learning, and trust. *Journal of School Leadership, 16*(5), 477–489.

Marshall, C., & Rossman, G. B. (2011). *Designing qualitative research* (5th ed.). Thousand Oaks, CA: SAGE.

Schechter, C. (2008b). Exploring success-based learning as an alternative instructional framework in principal preparatory programs. *Journal of School Leadership, 18*(1), 62–95.

Schechter, C. (2011a). Collective learning from success as perceived by school superintendents. *Journal of School Leadership, 21*(5), 478–509.

Schechter, C. (2011c). Towards communal negotiation of meaning in schools: Principals' perceptions of collective learning from success. *Teachers College Record, 113*(11), 2415–2459.

Schechter, C. (2015). Toward collective learning in schools: Exploring U.S.A. and Israeli teachers' perceptions of collective learning from success. *International Journal of Educational Reform, 24*(2), 160–184.

Schechter, C., & Michael, O. (2014). Intern teachers' and mentor teachers' perceptions regarding learning from success during the internship year. *Educational Practice and Theory, 36*(1), 57–81.

Sergiovanni, T. J. (2005). The virtues of leadership. *The Educational Forum, 69*, 112–123.

Sykes, I. J., Rosenfeld, J. M., & Weiss, Z. (2006). *Learning from success as a leverage for school-wide learning: The retrospective method.* Jerusalem, Israel: JDC-Brookdale.

CHAPTER 4

Argyris, C., & Schon, D. (1996). *Organizational learning II: Theory, method and practice.* Reading, MA: Addison-Wesley.

Ellenbogen-Frankovits, S., Shemer, O., & Rosenfeld, J. M. (2011). *Promoting organizational learning processes: A handbook introducing learning from success and ongoing learning.* Jerusalem, Israel: JDC-Brookdale.

Gino, F., & Pisano, G. P. (2011). Why leaders don't learn from success. *Harvard Business Review, 89*(4), 68–74.

Grimmett, P. P. (1988). The nature of reflection and Schon's conception in perspective. In P. P. Grimmett & G. L. Erickson (Eds.), *Reflection in teacher education* (pp. 5–16). New York, NY: Pacific Educational Press.

Hargreaves, A., & Fullan, M. (2012). *Professional capital: Transforming teaching in every school.* New York, NY: Teachers College Press.

Musca, C. (Producer), & Menendez, R. (Director). (1988). *Stand and deliver* [Motion picture]. United States: Warner Brothers.

Rosenfeld, J. M. (1996, September). *Learning from success: How to forge actionable knowledge for social work.* Opening lecture at the forum on learning from success. Alice Solomon, Facchochschule, Berlin, Germany.

Rosenfeld, J. M. (1997). Learning from success: How to design social work to be suitable for its purposes. *Social Welfare, 17*(4), 261–281.

Rosenfeld, J. M., & Krim, A. (1983). Adversity as opportunity: Urban families who did well after a fire. *Social Casework, 6*, 561–585.

Rosenfeld, J. M., Schon, D. A., & Sykes, I. J. (1995). *Out from under: Lessons from projects for inaptly served children and families.* Jerusalem, Israel: JDC-Brookdale.

Rosenfeld, J. M., Sykes, I. J., Weiss, Z., & Dolev, T. (2002). *Learning from success as leverage for school-wide learning.* Jerusalem, Israel: Ministry of Education Division of Secondary Education, with JDC-Brookdale.

Rosenfeld, J. M., & Tardieu, B. (2000). *Artisans of democracy: How ordinary people, families in extreme poverty, and social institutions become allies to overcome social exclusion.* New York, NY: University Press of America.

Schechter, C. (2010). Learning from success as a leverage for professional learning community: Exploring a school improvement process. *Teachers College Record, 112*(1), 180–224.

Schechter, C. (2012). Developing teachers' collective learning: Collective learning from success as perceived by three echelons in the school system. *International Journal of Educational Research, 56*, 60–74.

Schechter, C., Sykes, I., & Rosenfeld, J. (2008). Learning from success as leverage for school learning: Lessons from a national program. *International Journal of Leadership in Education, 11*(3), 301–318.

Sykes, I. J., Rosenfeld, J. M., & Weiss, Z. (2006). *Learning from success as a leverage for school-wide learning: The retrospective method.* Jerusalem, Israel: JDC-Brookdale.

CHAPTER 5

Bateson, G. (1972). *Steps to ecology of mind.* San Francisco, CA: Chandler Publishing.

Ellenbogen-Frankovits, S., Shemer, O., & Rosenfeld, J. M. (2011). *Promoting organizational learning processes: A handbook introducing learning from success and ongoing learning.* Jerusalem, Israel: JDC-Brookdale.

Organization for Economic Co-operation and Development [OECD]. (2016). *Education at a glance 2016: OECD indicators.* Paris, France: Author. Retrieved from http://www.oecd.org/edu/education-at-a-glance-19991487.htm

Schechter, C., Sykes, I., & Rosenfeld, J. (2008). Learning from success as leverage for school learning: Lessons from a national program. *International Journal of Leadership in Education, 11*(3), 301–318.

CHAPTER 6

Anderson, E., & Reynolds, A. L. (2015). *A policymaker's guide: Research-based policy for principal preparation program approval and licensure.* Charlottesville, VA: University Council of Educational Administration.

Coburn, C. E. (2016). What's policy got to do with it? How the structure-agency debate can illuminate policy implementation. *American Journal of Education, 122,* 465–475.

Cook, S., & Yanow, D. (1996). Culture and organizational learning. In M. Cohen & L. Sproull (Eds.), *Organizational learning* (pp. 403–429). Thousand Oaks, CA: SAGE.

Darling-Hammond, L., Meyerson, D., La Pointe, M., & Orr, M. T. (2010). *Preparing principals for a changing world: Lessons from effective school leadership programs.* San Francisco, CA: Jossey-Bass.

Diem, S., & Carpenter, B. W. (2013). Examining race-related silences: Interrogating the education of tomorrow's educational leaders. *Journal of Research on Leadership Education, 8*(1), 56–76.

Ellis, S., Mendel, R., & Nir, M. (2006). Learning from successful and failed experiences: The moderating role of a kind of after-event review. *Journal of Applied Psychology, 91*(3), 669–680.

Ganon-Shilon, S., & Schechter, C. (2017). Making sense of school leaders' sense-making. *Educational Management, Administration and Leadership, 45*(4), 682–698.

Ganon-Shilon, S., & Schechter, C. (2019). No school principal is an island: From individual to school sense-making processes in reform implementation. *Management in Education, 33*(2), 77–85.

Kurtz, K. J., Boukrina, O., & Gentner, D. (2013). Comparison promotes learning and transfer of relational categories. *Journal of Experimental Psychology: Learning, Memory, and Cognition, 39*(4), 1303–1310.

Madsen, P. M., & Desai, V. (2010). Failing to learn? The effects of failure and success on organizational learning in the global orbital launch vehicle industry. *Academy of Management Journal, 53*(3), 451–476.

Maitlis, S., & Christianson, M. (2014). Sensemaking in organizations: Taking stock and moving forward. *The Academy of Management Annals, 8*, 57–125.

Michalsky, T., & Schechter, C. (2013). Preservice teachers' self-regulated learning: Integrating learning from problems and learning from successes. *Teaching and Teacher Education, 30*(1), 60–73.

Michalsky, T., & Schechter, C. (2018). Teachers' self-regulated learning lesson design: Integrating learning from problems and successes. *The Teacher Educator, 53*(2), 101–123.

Nonaka, I. (1985). *The essence of failure: Can management learn from the manner of organization of Japanese military forces in the Pacific War?* Unpublished working paper. Institute of Business: Hitotsubashi University.

Pintrich, P. R. (2000). Multiple goals, multiple pathways: The role of goal orientation in learning and achievement. *Journal of Educational Psychology, 92*, 544–555.

Printy, S. (2008). Leadership for teacher learning: A community of practice perspective. *Educational Administration Quarterly, 44*(2), 187–226.

Schechter, C. (2001). Is this dialogue falling upon deaf ears? Exploring the deliberative process among school administrators. *Journal of School Leadership, 11*(6), 468–492.

Schechter, C. (2008). Exploring success-based learning as an alternative instructional framework in principal preparatory programs. *Journal of School Leadership, 18*(1), 62–95.

Schechter, C. (2011). Switching cognitive gears: Problem-based learning and success-based learning as an instructional framework in leadership education. *Journal of Educational Administration, 49*(2), 143–165.

Schechter, C., & Michalsky, T. (2014). Juggling our mindsets: Learning from success as a complementary instructional framework in teacher education. *Teachers College Record, 116*(2), 1–48.

Schechter, C., & Shaked, H. (2017). Leaving fingerprints: Principals' considerations while implementing education reforms. *Journal of Educational Administration, 55*(3), 242–260.

Shaked, H., & Schechter, C. (2018). Integrating learning from problems and learning from success in a principal preparation program. *Planning and Changing, 48*(1/2), 86–105.

Sitkin, S. (1996). Learning through failure: The strategy of small losses. In M. D. Cohen & L. S. Sproull (Eds.), *Organizational learning* (pp. 541–578). Thousand Oaks, CA: SAGE.

Smerek, R. E. (2011). Sensemaking and sensegiving: An exploratory study of the simultaneous "being and learning" of new college and university presidents. *Journal of Leadership and Organizational Studies, 18*, 80–94.

Sumbera, M. J., Pazey, B. L., & Lashley, C. (2014). How building principals made sense of free and appropriate public education in the least restrictive environment. *Leadership and Policy in Schools, 13*, 297–333.

Virany, B., Tushman, M., & Romanelli, E. (1996). Executive succession and organization outcomes in turbulent environments: An organizational learning approach. In M. D. Cohen & L. S. Sproull (Eds.), *Organizational learning* (pp. 302–329). Thousand Oaks, CA: SAGE.

Wallace Foundation. (2016). *Improving university principal preparation programs: Five themes from the field*. Retrieved from http://www.wallacefoundation.org/knowledge-center/Documents/Improving-University-Principal-Preparation-Programs.pdf

Weick, K. E. (2009). *Making sense of organization: Vol. 2. The impermanent organization*. Chichester, UK: Wiley.

Weiler, S. C., & Cray, M. (2012). Measuring Colorado superintendents' perceptions of principal preparation programs. *Educational Considerations, 39*(2), 66–76.

Wenger, E. (1998). *Communities of practice: Learning, meaning and identity*. Cambridge, UK: Cambridge University Press.

Williams, S. M. (2015). The future of principal preparation and principal evaluation: Reflections of the current policy context for school leaders. *Journal of Research on Leadership Education, 10*(3), 222–225.

Zimmerman, B. J. (2000). Attainment of self-regulated learning: A social cognitive perspective. In M. Boekaerts, P. Pintrich, & M. Zeidner (Eds.), *Handbook of self-regulation* (pp. 13–39). Orlando, FL: Academic Press.

Zimmerman, B. J. (2008). Investigating self-regulation and motivation: Historical background, methodological developments, and future prospects. *American Educational Research Journal, 45*(1), 166–183.

Index

A SAGE Publishing Company

Helping educators make the greatest impact

CORWIN HAS ONE MISSION: to enhance education through intentional professional learning.

We build long-term relationships with our authors, educators, clients, and associations who partner with us to develop and continuously improve the best evidence-based practices that establish and support lifelong learning.

THE PROFESSIONAL LEARNING ASSOCIATION

Learning Forward is a nonprofit, international membership association of learning educators committed to one vision in K–12 education: Excellent teaching and learning every day. To realize that vision, Learning Forward pursues its mission to build the capacity of leaders to establish and sustain highly effective professional learning. Information about membership, services, and products is available from www.learningforward.org.